P9-CRQ-402

BUCKINGHAM PALACE

OFFICIAL GUIDEBOOK

ROYAL COLLECTION PUBLICATIONS

Published by
Royal Collection Enterprises Ltd
St James's Palace
London
SW1A 1JR

For a complete catalogue of current publications, please write to the address above, or visit our website on www.royal.gov.uk

Text written by John Martin Robinson.
This edition revised by Royal Collection Enterprises Ltd, 2003.
© 2003 Royal Collection Enterprises Ltd
Text and reproductions of all items in the Royal Collection © 2003 HM Queen Elizabeth II

117929/03/1

All rights reserved. No part of this publication may be reproduced, stored in a retrieval system or transmitted in any form or by any means, whether electronic or mechanical, including photocopying, recording or otherwise, without prior permission in writing from the publisher.

ISBN 1 902163 60 5

British Library Cataloguing in Publication Data.
A catalogue record of this book is available from the British Library.

Designed by Baseline Arts Ltd, Oxford
Produced by Book Production Consultants plc, Cambridge
Printed and bound by Norwich Colour Print Ltd

The unique status of Buckingham Palace as a working royal palace means that paintings and works of art are sometimes moved at short notice. Pictures and works of art are also frequently lent from the Royal Collection to exhibitions all over the world. The arrangement of objects and paintings may therefore occasionally vary from that given in this guidebook.

For ticket and booking information on the Summer Opening of the state rooms at Buckingham Palace, please contact:
Ticket Sales and Information Office
Buckingham Palace
London SW1A 1AA

Credit card booking line: (+44) (0)20 7766 7300
Group bookings: (+44) (0)20 7766 7321
Fax: (+44) (0)20 7930 9625
Email: information@royalcollection.org.uk
groupbookings@royalcollection.org.uk
www.royal.gov.uk

CONTENTS

LEFT: Cleaning the chandeliers in the Music Room, as part of the regular maintenance of the state rooms.

FRONTISPIECE: Crowds outside the front of Buckingham Palace celebrate The Queen Mother's 100th birthday.

BUCKINGHAM PALACE

BUCKINGHAM PALACE is one of the official residences of Her Majesty The Queen. The Queen is Head of State of the United Kingdom of Great Britain and Northern Ireland, and Head of the Commonwealth. The Queen is also Head of State of sixteen of the Commonwealth's fifty-four member countries.

As a constitutional sovereign The Queen acts on the advice of her ministers; nevertheless, the Government, the judiciary and the armed services all act in The Queen's name and the monarch is the principal symbol of national unity. The Queen is kept closely informed about all aspects of national life

and the Prime Minister has a weekly audience with her at Buckingham Palace. The Queen also has certain residual 'prerogative' powers, which include the appointment of the Prime Minister and granting the dissolution of Parliament.

Many of The Queen's duties are ceremonial and a reminder of the long history of the United Kingdom. These duties include the State Opening of Parliament, The Queen's Birthday Parade (also known as Trooping the Colour), Garter Day celebrations of the Order of the Garter, which take place at Windsor Castle, and state visits overseas.

OPPOSITE ABOVE: The Queen and The Duke of Edinburgh with President Bush and Mrs Bush at Buckingham Palace in 2001.

OPPOSITE BELOW: The Queen with Audley Harrison, Steven Redgrave and Denise Lewis at a reception held at Buckingham Palace for Britain's 2000 Olympic team.

Buckingham Palace serves as the office and official home for The Queen as well as the administrative headquarters for the Royal Household. It is the setting for state ceremonies and official entertaining and is one of the few working royal palaces remaining in the world today. This gives it a particular fascination. The Queen, as Head of State, receives a large number of formal and informal visitors there, including the Privy Council, foreign and British high commissioners and ambassadors, members of the clergy, and senior officers of the armed services and the civil service. There are regular investitures in the Ballroom and each autumn The Queen gives a splendid formal reception in the state rooms for all members of the diplomatic corps in London. At least three garden parties are held in the summer, attended by a wide range of guests drawn from all walks of life and amounting to more than 27,000 people. The Queen also holds small lunch parties for guests drawn from leaders in the community.

The highlight of royal entertaining, however, is the state banquet, usually for about 170 guests, given by The Queen on the first evening of a state visit by a foreign head of state to the United Kingdom. At Buckingham Palace, state banquets are held in the Ballroom, the largest of the state rooms, using the magnificent gold plate from the Royal Collection, much of it made for George IV. Guests are received in the Music Room and a royal procession is formed to the Ballroom, led by The Queen and the visiting head of state and preceded by the Lord Chamberlain and the Lord Steward.

The state rooms, which form the backdrop to the pageantry of court ceremonial and official entertaining, occupy the main west block of Buckingham Palace, facing the gardens. In all, Buckingham Palace has 19 state rooms, 52 royal and guest bedrooms, 188 staff bedrooms, 92 offices and 78 bathrooms. Some 450 people work in the palace and more than 50,000 people are entertained there every year, while the Summer Opening of the state rooms, which began in 1993, has attracted more than 3 million visitors from all over the world.

The head of the Royal Household is the Lord Chamberlain. Under him are the heads of five departments: the Private Secretary; the Comptroller of the Lord Chamberlain's Office, who is in charge of ceremonial; the Keeper of the Privy Purse, who runs royal finances; the Master of the Household, a position dating back to 1539, who is responsible for the organisation of official entertaining; and the Director of the Royal Collection.

Within Buckingham Palace and throughout the royal palaces, incomparable works of art from the Royal Collection are displayed in the historic setting for which they were collected or commissioned by successive monarchs.

Illustrated Timeline

THIS TIMELINE SHOWS some of the most significant developments in the history of Buckingham Palace from its beginnings in the 17th century to the present day.

1633
Lord Goring builds a 'fair house and other convenient buildings and outhouses' on the site of Buckingham Palace

1665
Lord Goring's house let to 'Mr Secretary Bennet', later the Earl of Arlington

1675
Lord Goring's house destroyed by fire

1677
Lord Goring's house rebuilt as Arlington House

1698
Palace of Whitehall destroyed by fire; court moves to St James's Palace

1702-05
Arlington House rebuilt for the Duke of Buckingham

1761
Buckingham House acquired for the Crown as a private residence by George III

1762-74
Buckingham House remodelled by Sir William Chambers

1826
George IV begins remodelling Buckingham House

1827
Parliamentary Select Committee into the expense of the remodelling of Buckingham Palace and other public buildings in London

STUART	COMMONWEALTH	STUART				HANOVER			
CHARLES I	PROTECTORATE	CHARLES II	JAMES II	WILLIAM III & MARY II	ANNE	GEORGE I	GEORGE II	GEORGE III	GEORGE IV
1625-1649	1649-1659	1660-1685	1685-1688	1689-1702	1702-14	1714-1727	1727-1760	1760-1820	1820-1830

1831
John Nash sacked for financial mismanagement, Edward Blore appointed as palace architect

1840
Queen Victoria marries Prince Albert of Saxe-Coburg

1847-50
Fourth side of palace quadrangle completed to house Queen Victoria and Prince Albert's growing family

1861
Death of Prince Albert

1902
Palace redecorated in white and gold under King Edward VII

1911-14
East front refaced, Picture Gallery redesigned

1914-18
First World War

1924
Entrée redecorated under King George V

1939-45
Second World War – palace bombed during the Blitz

1947
Wedding of Princess Elizabeth (now Queen Elizabeth II) to Prince Philip, The Duke of Edinburgh

1962
The Queen's Gallery at Buckingham Palace opened

1977
Queen Elizabeth II's Silver Jubilee

1993
State rooms at Buckingham Palace open to the public for the first time

THE QUEEN'S GOLDEN JUBILEE 2002

2002
Queen Elizabeth II's Golden Jubilee; Queen's Gallery rebuilt and reopened

		SAXE-COBURG GOTHA	WINDSOR				
WILLIAM IV	VICTORIA	EDWARD VII	GEORGE V	EDWARD VIII	GEORGE VI	ELIZABETH II
1830-1837	*1837-1901*	*1901-1910*	*1910-1936*	*1936*	*1936-1952*	*1952-*

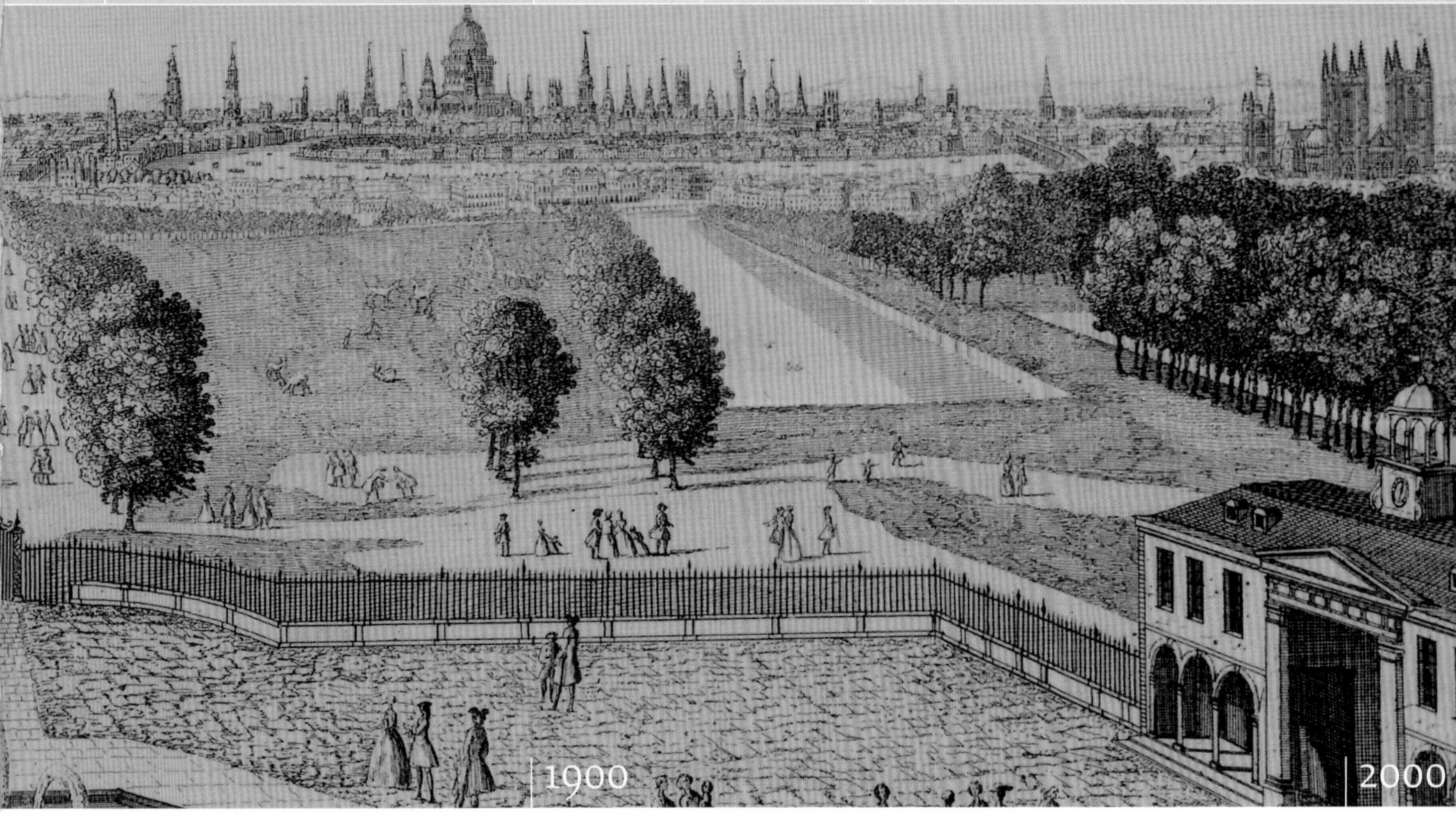

The view from Buckingham House in an engraving of 1794. The spires of the City churches and the dome of St Paul's are visible in the distance, with St James's Park in the foreground.

HISTORICAL INTRODUCTION

ABOVE: George, Lord Goring (1608–57). A nineteenth-century copy by an unknown artist of an earlier miniature.

DURING THE MIDDLE AGES the London residence of the Norman and Plantagenet kings and their successors was the Palace of Westminster, now rebuilt as the Houses of Parliament. Whitehall was the main royal palace from the reign of Henry VIII (r.1509-47) to that of William III (r.1689-1702), when it was largely destroyed by fire. In the eighteenth century St James's Palace, built by Henry VIII to serve as a hunting lodge in St James's Park, was used by the Hanoverian kings. But the creation of Buckingham Palace, as an appropriate symbol of national greatness in the aftermath of the victories of the Napoleonic Wars, was due to George IV (r.1820-30).

Although converted to a palace by George IV and first lived in by Queen Victoria soon after her accession in 1837, the property had originally been acquired for the Crown by George III. The history of the site, however, can be traced back

ABOVE: Arlington House (rebuilt as Buckingham House in 1702-05).

OPPOSITE ABOVE: Buckingham House in 1710.

OPPOSITE BELOW: Detail of a map of the Cities of London and Westminster, 1799, by Richard Horwood, showing Buckingham House (in red, left of centre) between The Queen's Gardens and St James's Park.

to the beginning of the seventeenth century. In 1633 Lord Goring built on it 'a fair house and other convenient buildings and outhouses'. This house was then rebuilt for Henry Bennett, Earl of Arlington, in 1677, and again for John Sheffield, Duke of Buckingham, in 1702-05 by the architect William Winde.

The most attractive feature of the house was its setting between St James's Park and Hyde Park, at the head of an avenue of limes and elms, with views towards Westminster and the City of London and with the dome of St Paul's Cathedral visible in the distance. It was more a country house on the edge of London than a town house, and to some extent it has retained this character.

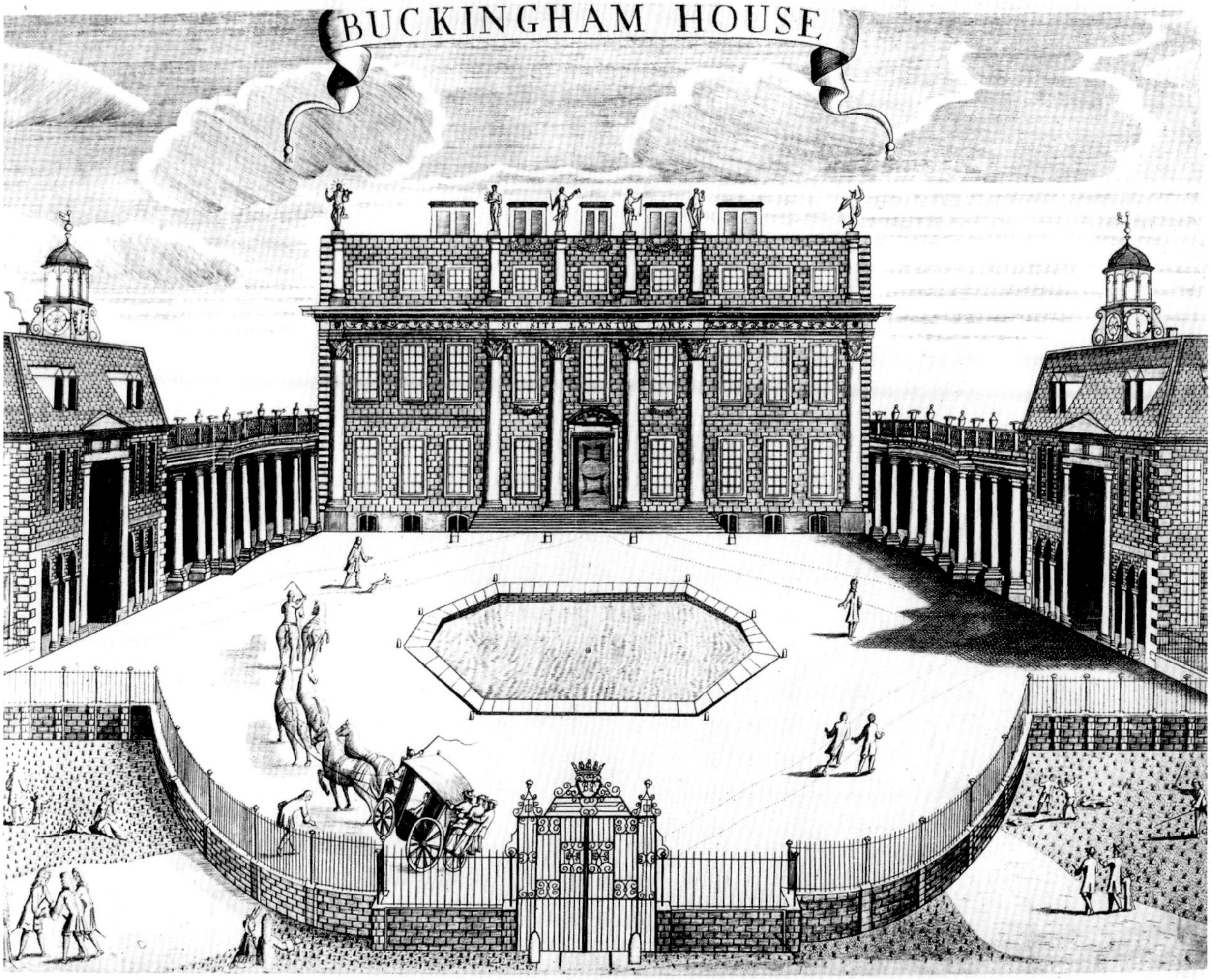
BUCKINGHAM HOUSE
SIC SITI LAETANTUR LARES

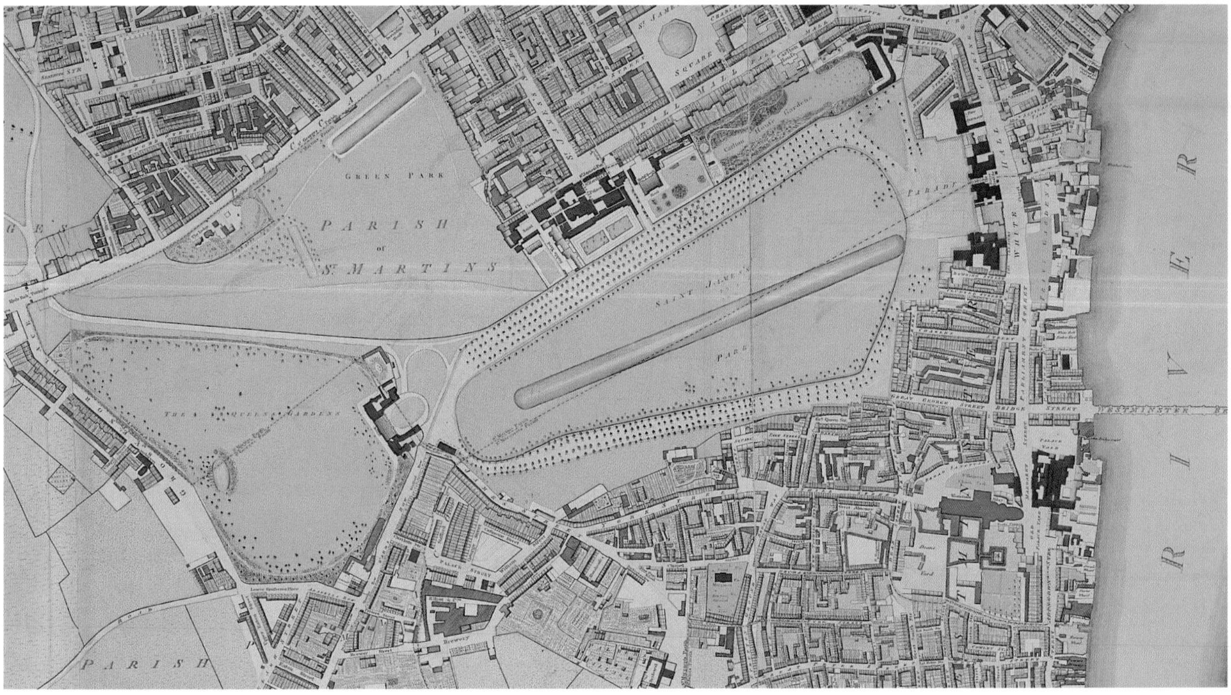
GREEN PARK
PARISH
of
St. MARTINS
SAINT JAMES'S
PARK
PARADE
PALL MALL
SQUARE
WHITE HALL
PARLIAMENT STREET
GREAT GEORGE STREET
BRIDGE STREET
WESTMINSTER
PALACE STREET
YORK STREET
PARISH
RIVER

ABOVE: Buckingham House as it was in 1819, in a watercolour by William Westall. George III simplified the façade of the Duke of Buckingham's house and added substantially to the north and south sides.

RIGHT: John Nash, architect of Buckingham Palace (1752–1835), in a pencil sketch of 1830 by Sir Edwin Landseer.

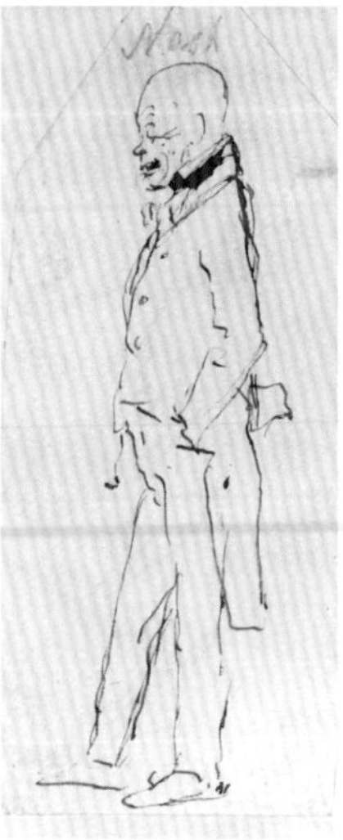

Buckingham House remained the property of the Dukes of Buckingham – after whom it was named – until the mid-eighteenth century. A problem over the lease of the property, half of which was on Crown land, enabled George III, who married Charlotte of Mecklenburg-Strelitz in 1761, to acquire the house outright in the same year as their private residence. Between 1762 and 1774 Buckingham House was remodelled by Sir William Chambers, but the ceremonial centre of the court remained at St James's. This is the reason that foreign ambassadors are still accredited to the Court of St James more than two centuries later.

When George IV came to the throne in 1820, he initially decided to adapt Buckingham House as his own private residence for use in conjunction with St James's, as in his father's day, but by 1826 he had opted instead to convert it into a royal palace where he could hold his courts and conduct the official business of the monarchy.

George IV chose as his architect John Nash, whose design for the new palace was theatrical and French-inspired, perfectly reflecting George IV's personal taste. Nash was hampered, however, by the King's ambivalence over the purpose of the palace – whether it was to be a private royal residence or a state palace – as well as by a shortage of funds. He was forced to keep and remodel the old house, and to this day the shell of the Duke of Buckingham's and George III's house is incorporated in the middle of the principal range of the palace, where it dictates the plan and dimensions of the rooms and the proportions of the ground floor.

Nash's plan was nevertheless an ingenious solution to a difficult architectural problem. The main block was doubled in size by the addition of new rooms on the garden side, while the old wings of the palace were substantially extended and enlarged to form a solid U-shape, enclosing an open courtyard. The open fourth side was finished with iron railings and a central triumphal arch (the Marble Arch now at the top of Park Lane). The old main block was remodelled, permitting both a circuit of the state rooms and a direct approach to the Throne Room within the original shell of the Duke of

BELOW: Johann Zoffany, *George III, Queen Charlotte and their six eldest children*, 1770. George III, his father Frederick, Prince of Wales, and his son George IV were responsible for the acquisition of many of the finest Old Master paintings and other works of art on display at Buckingham Palace.

Joseph Nash, *Buckingham Palace from the south east*, 1846. The Marble Arch, now at the top of Park Lane, can be seen here in its original position at the entrance to the forecourt.

Buckingham's house. This made the new state rooms on the first floor equally suitable for formal audiences and for more social court events.

The exterior of Nash's palace, faced in Bath stone, is exquisitely detailed in a French neo-classical manner, making much use of sculptured panels and trophies, while the main feature of the garden front was an enormous domed bow-window, reaching from the ground to the first floor.

The interiors of the palace were progressively enriched by George IV, guided by his artistic adviser Sir Charles Long, to meet an increasing desire for opulence and grandeur. The decoration was notable for its large-scale use of brightly coloured scagliola (imitation marble); its colour schemes of lapis blue and raspberry pink; the sculptured plaster panels set high on the walls; and the elaborately decorated ceilings. However George IV died before the rooms were finished, and the following year (1831) Nash was dismissed for financial incompetence.

The completion of the palace was then entrusted by William IV to Edward Blore, a more businesslike but less inspired architect. In general he kept to the lines of Nash's design, but made it more solid and less picturesque.

LEFT: Sir Thomas Lawrence, *George IV*, 1821. The Table of the Grand Commanders (see page 62), one of the treasures of the Royal Collection, can be seen on the left of the painting.

William IV never lived in Buckingham Palace, though it was completed in his reign. In 1837, when Queen Victoria moved in, the palace was fresh from the hands of the builders, but its inadequacies became obvious following the Queen's

ABOVE: Franz Xaver Winterhalter, *The Royal Family in 1846*. Queen Victoria, Prince Albert and their five eldest children.

LEFT: The Prince of Wales (later King Edward VII) photographed with friends in the garden of Buckingham Palace in 1854. He is seated on the right of the bench, with his brother Prince Alfred on the left. Lord Arthur Clinton sits between them.

marriage to her cousin, Prince Albert of Saxe-Coburg, in 1840. The palace was too small either for state functions or for family life. Splendid though George IV's state apartments were, none of them was big enough for a court ball. Equally difficult for the newly-married couple was the absence of nurseries. The obvious solution was to make the palace a complete quadrangle by closing in the open east side of the courtyard with a new wing. This scheme was adopted, entailing the removal of Nash's Marble Arch (see page 15).

This new range, with apartments for distinguished visitors on the first floor and nurseries above, was designed by Edward Blore and built by Thomas Cubitt from 1847 to 1850. The extension of the suite of state apartments along the west front of the palace by the addition of new galleries, the Ball Supper Room and the huge Ballroom, was entrusted to a different architect – Nash's pupil James Pennethorne. Prince Albert directed the redecoration of many of the principal rooms in consultation with an art-historian and professor from Dresden, Dr Ludwig Gruner.

During the long years of her widowhood Queen Victoria lived for the most part at Windsor Castle, and Buckingham Palace remained dark and shuttered for much of each year. When King Edward VII came to the throne in 1901, he considered the redecoration of the palace 'a duty and necessity'. The Ballroom, Grand Entrance, Marble Hall, Grand Staircase, vestibules and galleries were all painted white, heavily gilded, and embellished with festoons, swags and other decorative motifs at odds with Nash's original detailing.

For the east range Blore had used soft Caen stone which proved to be perishable in the London climate. In 1913, as part of the Queen Victoria Memorial, the Blore front was refaced in Portland stone to a new design by Sir Aston Webb. A remodelled approach to the palace along the Mall, originally planned in 1901, was completed at the same time. Much of the architectural grandeur comes from the forecourt and the *rond point* of the Victoria Memorial in front. The palace's magnificent iron and gilded bronze gates, made by the Bromsgrove Guild of Metalworkers in 1913-14, complete its impact for the visitor.

ABOVE: Sir Luke Fildes, *King Edward VII*, 1901

Plan of the State Rooms

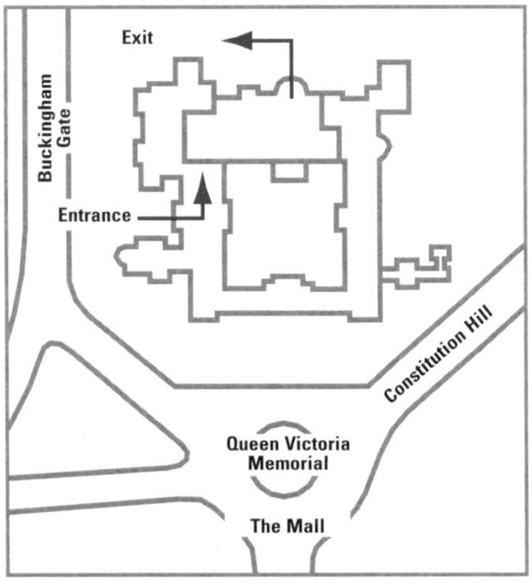

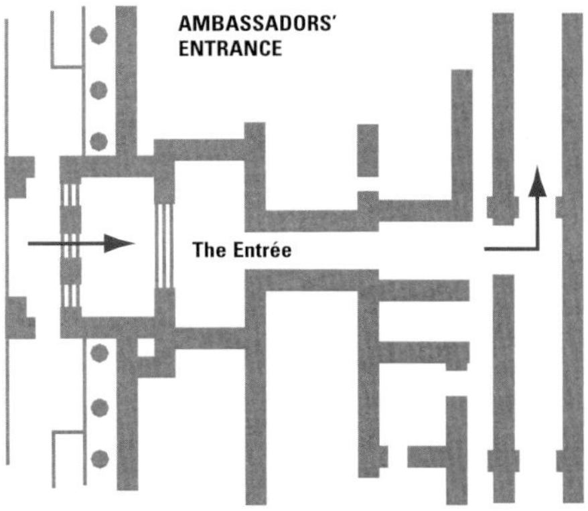

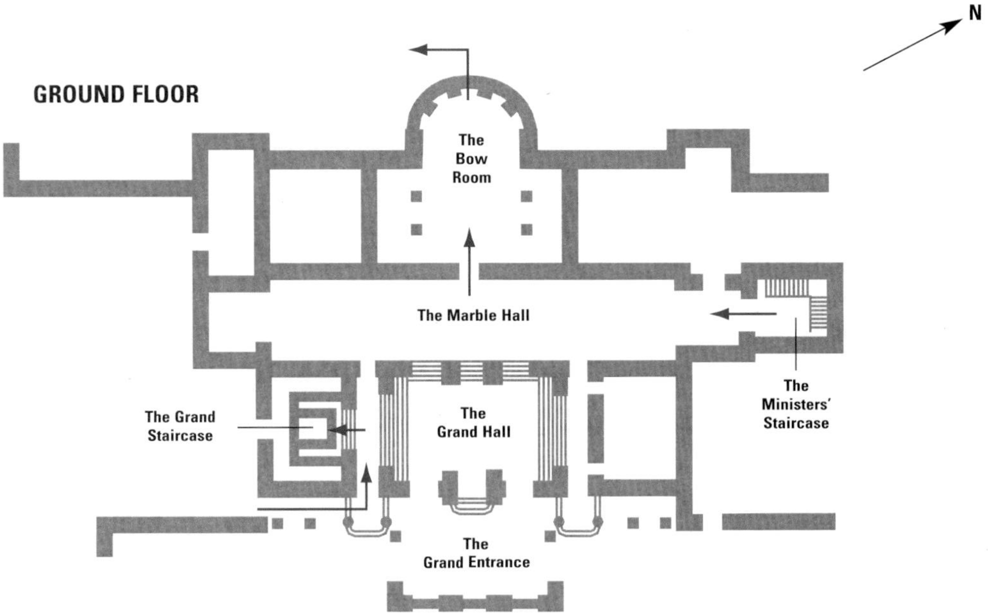

The Tour

VISITORS ENTER BUCKINGHAM PALACE through the Ambassadors' Court in the south wing. They go up the Grand Staircase to the first floor, and move through the state rooms from the Guard Room to the Picture Gallery. These are followed by the East Gallery, Ball Supper Room and Ballroom. Visitors then enter the rooms on the garden side of the palace. The Ministers' Staircase takes them back down to the ground floor, where they enter the garden via the Marble Hall and the Bow Room. Visitors leave the palace through the gardens and go out by Stonemason's Gate.

The Queen's private apartments are in the north wing of the palace, and suites of rooms for important visitors occupy the main floor of the east wing, facing the Mall. Much of the ground floor of the palace is occupied by the offices of the Royal Household, and the kitchens are in the south wing.

Room plans are provided for each of the state rooms, and give details of the paintings and works of art to be found in them.

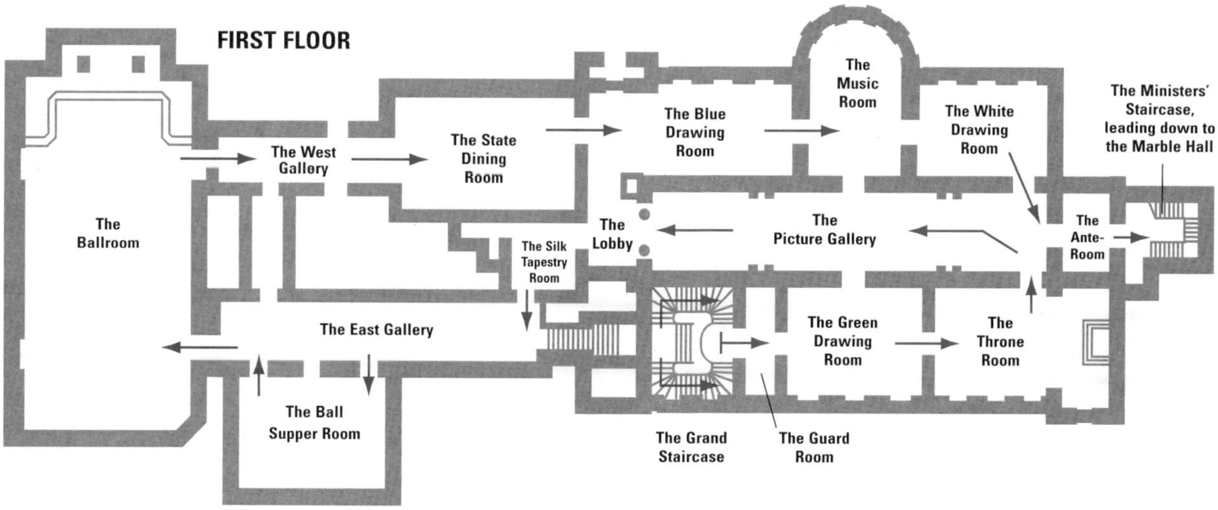

THE AMBASSADORS' ENTRANCE

The Order of the Garter

The Order of the Garter was founded by Edward III in 1348. The Garter ceremony, involving The Queen, The Duke of Edinburgh, other members of the Royal Family and the Knights of the Garter, still takes place every year in St George's Chapel, Windsor.

Symbols of the Order of the Garter, including the Garter itself and Garter Stars, can be found throughout the state rooms of Buckingham Palace and Windsor Castle.

LEFT: The Ambassadors' Entrance is used on official occasions by diplomats and others, as well as by visitors to the Buckingham Palace Summer Opening.

THE AMBASSADORS' ENTRANCE is a temple-like Ionic portico of Bath stone on the south side of the palace. It was added under the direction of Edward Blore after Nash had been dismissed, but takes its cue from the Nash pavilions on the garden front of the palace. (Visitors see the pavilions as they leave the palace via the gardens.)

Inside the entrance the hall itself is a narrow space, known as the Entrée, lined with marbled pilasters. The Brocatello marble chimneypiece and the mirror over it are insertions in the seventeenth-century style dating from 1924, when the Entrée was redecorated; they bear the monogram of King George V. The mirror incorporates a gilded sunburst clock, its dial encircled by the Garter.

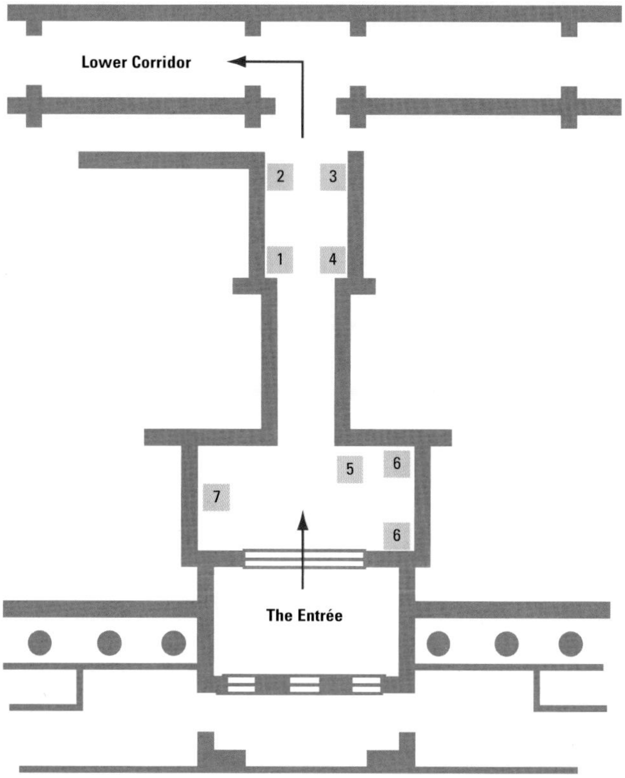

PICTURES

1 John Shackleton, *George II*, 1757
2 George Wilhelm Fountaine, *George I*, c.1725
3 Sir George Hayter, *Queen Victoria*, c.1840
4 British School, *Frederick, Prince of Wales*, c.1745

SCULPTURE

5 John McCombe Reynolds, bronze bust of HM The Queen, 1984

PORCELAIN

6 Pair of Chinese celadon vases, with gilt-bronze mounts by the firm of Benjamin Lewis Vulliamy, clockmakers and metalworkers, c.1810.

7 Chinese *famille rose* cistern, with gilt-bronze mounts by Benjamin Lewis Vulliamy, c.1820.

ABOVE: Members of the royal family watch from the Balcony on the front of the palace as the Duke and Duchess of York (later King George V and Queen Mary) leave Buckingham Palace to start their honeymoon, 6 July 1893. Queen Victoria can be seen seated in the centre; other guests watch from the windows.

LEFT: The Balcony in 2001: The Queen, The Duke of Edinburgh, The Queen Mother, The Prince of Wales and the Earl and Countess of Wessex after the annual Trooping the Colour ceremony.

The Grand Entrance

Turning left, visitors enter the Lower Corridor, which leads them round the side of the Quadrangle. It also allows the visitor to see the rear elevation of the front of the Palace. This may appear to have been built of golden Bath stone, in keeping with the rest of the Quadrangle, but is in fact painted stucco. The lower columns of the portico, through which visitors pass on their way up to the Grand Hall, are made of cast iron, also painted to resemble stone.

The visitor is also able to see something of the programme of sculptural ornament which was an important feature of the original design of the palace. John Flaxman (1755-1826), the greatest of English neo-classical sculptors, was approached to design a programme of external sculptural decoration. After his death his sketches were used by other sculptors; for example William Croggan, who supplied the capitals and friezes in artificial Coade stone in 1827.

BELOW: King George VI and Queen Elizabeth inspecting bomb damage at Buckingham Palace in April 1940. The palace was an obvious target for enemy bombing raids, and was hit several times. The Victorian private chapel in Nash's south-west pavilion on the garden front was heavily damaged. In 1962 this became The Queen's Gallery, and is now the Nash Gallery in the new enlarged Queen's Gallery on the same site.

The Grand Hall

The Chimneypiece

The chimneypiece at the north end of the Grand Hall, facing the Grand Staircase, is among the finest in the palace. It was supplied in 1829, at a cost of £1,000, by Joseph Theakston, 'the ablest carver of his time', and its design shows the influence of Napoleon's architects Charles Percier and Pierre Fontaine. At the top is a small bust of George IV.

THE GRAND HALL is of the same dimensions as the hall of the old Buckingham House and retains its low proportions, stressing that this is a sub-storey, with the main rooms above on a *piano nobile*, as in an Italian Renaissance palace. The spatial qualities of the room are considerably enhanced by the use of rich materials – the floor and Corinthian columns are all of white Carrara marble, supplied to Nash by Joseph Browne, who was sent to Italy to procure it, while the Corinthian capitals, which were supplied by Samuel Parker, are of gilded bronze.

Originally the marmoreal quality of the hall was further enhanced by the treatment of the walls, which included panels of coloured scagliola. The present white and gold decoration was executed by C. H. Bessant in 1902 for King Edward VII.

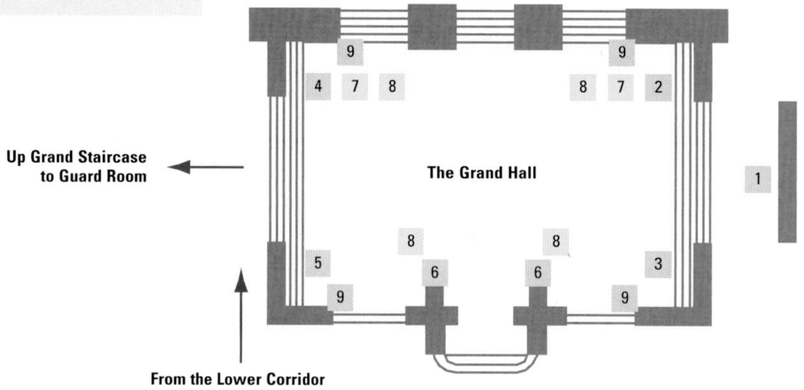

SCULPTURE

1 Chimneypiece and overmantel by Joseph Theakston, 1829.

2 Richard James Wyatt, *Nymph of Diana*, c.1850; completed by John Gibson and Benjamin Edward Spence after Wyatt's death.

3 Wolf von Hoyer, *Psyche with a lamp*, 1851

4 Pietro Tenerani, *Flora*, 1848

5 William Theed, *Psyche lamenting the loss of Cupid*, 1847

6 Pair of French granite urns with patinated and gilt-bronze mounts, purchased by George IV in 1828 for Windsor Castle.

FURNITURE

7 Set of hall chairs and benches made by Elward, Marsh & Tatham for the Hall at the Royal Pavilion, Brighton. Mahogany painted with Prince of Wales feathers, 1802.

8 Set of chairs, mahogany and gilt with tapering backs, (later painted with Queen Victoria's cypher), c.1790; made for the Hall at Carlton House, London.

PORCELAIN

9 Set of four Spode porcelain cisterns with gilt-bronze mounts attributed to Benjamin Lewis Vulliamy, c.1820.

THE GRAND HALL. John Nash created dramatic spatial effects by lowering the floor of the central area, with vistas across the different levels into the adjoining spaces, and agreeable contrasts of light and shade.

George IV and Carlton House

Some of the mahogany seat furniture, hall chairs and benches in the Grand Hall were originally made for George IV when he was Prince of Wales, and come from Carlton House. This building stood facing St James's Park, at the other end of The Mall from the palace, and was the Prince's London home until its demolition around 1827. (The site is now occupied by Nash's Carlton House Terrace and by the column commemorating the Duke of York.)

Detail of the painted decoration of one of the mahogany benches in the Grand Hall.

Carlton House was demolished when George IV decided to move to Buckingham Palace, but its magnificent fittings, furniture and works of art – the product of nearly forty years' discerning patronage on the part of the Prince – were all moved to Buckingham Palace and Windsor Castle. Throughout the state rooms at Buckingham Palace, the visitor will notice magnificent chandeliers, French and English furniture, and paintings which George IV originally acquired for Carlton House. In fact, the state rooms were partly designed round his collection and were conceived as a magnificent setting for these superlative works of art.

THE GRAND STAIRCASE AND GUARD ROOM

THE GRAND STAIRCASE IS ONE OF THE PRINCIPAL ARCHITECTURAL FEATURES OF THE PALACE

THE PLASTER DECORATIONS WERE INFLUENCED BY THOSE DESIGNED BY PERCIER AND FONTAINE FOR THE EMPEROR NAPOLEON

THE ARRANGEMENT OF PORTRAITS ON THE GRAND STAIRCASE WAS DEVISED BY QUEEN VICTORIA

THE SPATIAL COMPLEXITY of the Grand Hall is continued in the Grand Staircase, where Nash contrived an almost baroque vista, with the stairs continuing in one straight flight from the half-landing as well as returning in two arms along the sides. This plan was an ingenious arrangement to enable the state rooms to be approached from two directions – one could pass through all the state rooms in turn or approach the Throne Room directly. The staircase is on the same site as those of the two previous houses, but it is a complete rebuilding by Nash for George IV. It also provides a dramatic transition to the state rooms on the first floor. Light floods down from the etched glass dome by Wainwright & Brothers, the patterns on which are reminiscent of white damask.

The staircase itself is of Carrara marble, and the sumptuous gilt-bronze balustrade, embellished with rich Grecian foliage, is reflected in the design of the plaster string-course round the walls. It was made by Samuel Parker in 1828–30 at a cost of £3,900 and is the finest of its type in England. Parker also provided the gilt-

LEFT: The Grand Staircase.

RIGHT: Eugène Lami, *State Ball at Buckingham Palace, 5 July 1848*. This watercolour shows Nash's Grand Staircase of the late 1820s with its balustrade by Samuel Parker and Gruner's polychrome wall decoration of 1845.

THE GUARD ROOM. At Buckingham Palace this room is more symbolic than useful, but though small, it is one of Nash's most successful spaces at the palace. With its apsed ends, Carrara marble columns and richly decorated plaster ceiling by Bernasconi it forms an architectural overture to the glories to come.

metal mounts for the unique mahogany-framed, mirror-plated doors designed by Nash and used throughout the state rooms, adding enormously to their glittering spaciousness.

The walls of the Grand Staircase, which are now white and gold, were originally covered with more polychrome panels of scagliola. The sculptural decorations in moulded plaster survive and, like the chimneypiece in the Grand Hall, were influenced by Percier and Fontaine's palace interiors for Napoleon. In the Grand Staircase they were designed by the painter Thomas Stothard (1755–1834). The long rectangular reliefs of the Four Seasons were executed by his son Alfred Stothard, while the reliefs of cupids in the lunettes were modelled by Francis Bernasconi (*fl.* 1800-1835), the leading plasterer at the palace.

For reasons of space, the formal approach to the Throne Room is much abridged from the traditional sequence in English palaces (still to be seen at its full extent in the state rooms at Hampton Court Palace). At Buckingham Palace it comprises only the small Guard Room, the Green Drawing Room and the Throne Room itself.

The white marble neo-classical statues, including life-size portraits of herself and Prince Albert, were placed here by Queen Victoria. The glass chandelier, like those throughout the state rooms, comes from Carlton House.

The Guard Room is too small to accommodate the ceremonial guards used on formal occasions, who are deployed instead in the adjoining rooms. They are composed of two corps. One is the Yeomen of the Guard – the royal bodyguard, initiated by Henry VII in 1485 and the oldest bodyguard in the world, who still wear picturesque Tudor uniform. The other is the Gentlemen-at-Arms, founded by Henry VIII in 1537, who wear magnificent scarlet and gold uniforms in a nineteenth-century style, with plumed helmets of polished steel.

THE GRAND STAIRCASE

FITTINGS

1 Balustrade supplied by Samuel Parker, 1828–30.

SCULPTURE

2 Jan Geefs, *Love and Malice*, 1859; a birthday present from Queen Victoria to Prince Albert, 26 August 1859.

3 Richard James Wyatt, *The Huntress*, 1850; a birthday present from Queen Victoria to Prince Albert, 26 August 1850.

4 Bronze 19th-century copy of Benvenuto Cellini's *Perseus and Medusa* from the Loggia dei Lanzi, Florence.

PORCELAIN

5 Four Chinese porcelain vases with gilt-bronze mounts, early 19th century; they may have been purchased by George IV from the dealer Robert Fogg in 1823 for £520.

6 Two large Chinese *famille rose* baluster vases.

PICTURES

Portraits of Queen Victoria's immediate ancestors and relations, illustrating her succession; an installation devised for Queen Victoria shortly after her Coronation in 1838. Looking upwards from the half-landing the portraits are viewed clockwise from:

7 Sir Thomas Lawrence, *William IV*, 1827

8 Sir Thomas Lawrence, *Prince George of Cumberland* (later George V, King of Hanover), 1828

9 George Dawe, *Princess Charlotte of Wales*, 1817

10 George Dawe, *Leopold I, King of the Belgians*, 1844

11 Sir William Beechey, *Queen Charlotte*, 1796

12 Sir William Beechey, *George III*, 1799–1800

13 Sir George Hayter, *Victoria, Duchess of Kent*, 1835

14 Sir David Wilkie, *Augustus, Duke of Sussex*, 1833

15 George Dawe, *Edward, Duke of Kent*, 1818

16 Sir Martin Archer Shee, *Queen Adelaide*, 1836

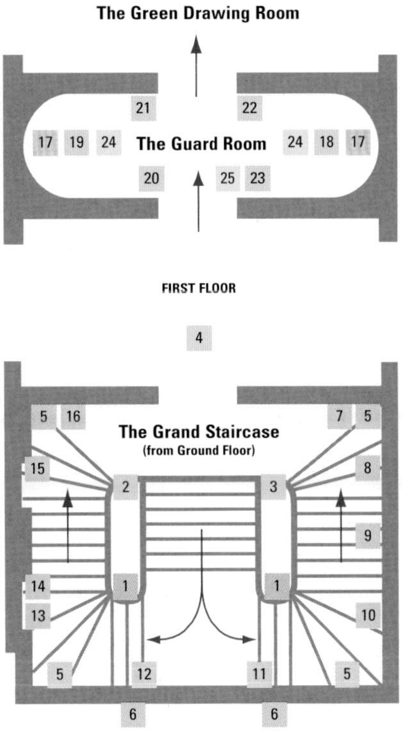

THE GUARD ROOM

TAPESTRIES

17 Two 18th-century Gobelins tapestries from the series *Les Portières des Dieux: Venus* symbolising spring (left); *Bacchus* symbolising autumn (right); and four narrow strips of tapestry known as *entrefenêtres*.

SCULPTURE

18 John Gibson, *Queen Victoria*, 1847; originally partly tinted.

19 Emil Wolff, *Prince Albert*, 1846; a replica of the original now at Osborne House, Isle of Wight. The Prince is dressed in ancient Greek costume.

20 Mary Thornycroft, *Princesses Victoria and Maud of Wales*, 1877

21 Benjamin Edward Spence, *Lady of the Lake*, 1861; a birthday present from Queen Victoria to Prince Albert, 26 August 1861.

22 Benjamin Edward Spence, *Highland Mary*, 1853; a birthday present from Prince Albert to Queen Victoria, 24 May 1853.

23 Mary Thornycroft, *Princess Louise of Wales*, 1877

FURNITURE

24 Set of chairs by Morel & Seddon, 1826–8; made for Windsor Castle.

25 Chandelier, probably supplied by Parker & Perry, c.1811, for Carlton House.

THE GREEN DRAWING ROOM

GUESTS AND OFFICIAL VISITORS GATHER IN THE GREEN DRAWING ROOM BEFORE BEING PRESENTED TO THE QUEEN

THIS ROOM CONTAINS SOME FINE EXAMPLES OF GEORGE IV'S COLLECTION OF FRENCH FURNITURE AND WORKS OF ART

THE GREEN DRAWING ROOM forms the ante-room to the Throne Room. It occupies the site of both the original saloon of Buckingham House and the later saloon of Queen Charlotte, which had been redesigned by Sir William Chambers. It retains the latter's dimensions, rising through two storeys to a high coved ceiling, but was entirely remodelled by Nash for George IV. The room still keeps to a large extent the original character of Nash's architecture, with green silk wall hangings framed by lattice-patterned pilasters, the work of the plasterer George Jackson.

The ceiling of this room is the first in a series of extraordinary ceiling designs created by Nash for the palace. They develop the tent-like 'Mogul' themes originally explored by him at the Royal Pavilion, Brighton; and with their billowing curves and domes are a unique feature of the state rooms. *Fraser's Magazine* commented in 1830:

> *It is, indeed, not easy to conceive anything more splendid than the designs for ceilings which are to be finished in a style new in this country, partaking very much of the boldest style in the Italian taste of the fifteenth century ... they will present the effect of embossed gold ornaments.*

The details and motifs are derived from a wide range of sources, including the Italian Renaissance as well as Classical Greece and Rome, and stretch the canon of Georgian taste to the limits. The carved marble chimneypieces are part of a series supplied for the palace by Joseph Browne between 1827 and 1830 at a cost of £6,000.

SÈVRES SOFT-PASTE PORCELAIN POT-POURRI VASE, 1758. This probably originally belonged to Madame de Pompadour, Louis XV's mistress. During 2003 it can be seen in the *Royal Treasures* exhibition at The Queen's Gallery, Buckingham Palace.

Sèvres Porcelain at Buckingham Palace

The magnificent Sèvres porcelain in the Green Drawing Room and throughout the state rooms was collected by George IV. Now divided between Buckingham Palace and Windsor Castle, it forms the finest group of Sèvres porcelain in the world, much of it of French royal provenance. During the French Revolution the contents of the palaces of France were systematically sold and many of the finer pieces were bought by English collectors. Chief among these was George IV, who as Prince of Wales, Regent and King employed a series of agents in Paris to acquire suitable objects for Carlton House and later for his new rooms at Windsor Castle and Buckingham Palace. Much of his incomparable collection remains in the settings for which he intended it. The Sèvres pot-pourri vase seen here, for example, was bought in Paris in 1817 by George IV's agent François Benois and cost 2,500 francs.

The state rooms at Buckingham Palace were not completed at the time of George IV's death. Their decoration was continued during the reign of William IV by Viscount Duncannon, the government minister responsible for Crown buildings. As well as the contents of Carlton House, Duncannon brought in additional pieces from Windsor Castle. For example the gilt seat furniture in the Green Drawing Room is part of a huge set made by Morel & Seddon in 1826–8 for the semi-state rooms at Windsor Castle, while the fluted pedestals for candelabra came from the Throne Room at Carlton House. The Green Drawing Room now also contains examples of George IV's finest pieces of French furniture, including a cabinet by Adam Weisweiler embellished with superb seventeenth-century *pietra dura* panels.

CABINET WITH *PIETRA DURA* PANELS by Adam Weisweiler, c.1780-85. It is enriched with 17th-century panels of *pietra dura*; some, such as the two with single flowers, may have been made in Florence. Those in relief may have come from the Gobelins manufactory. It was probably bought by George IV for Carlton House in 1791.

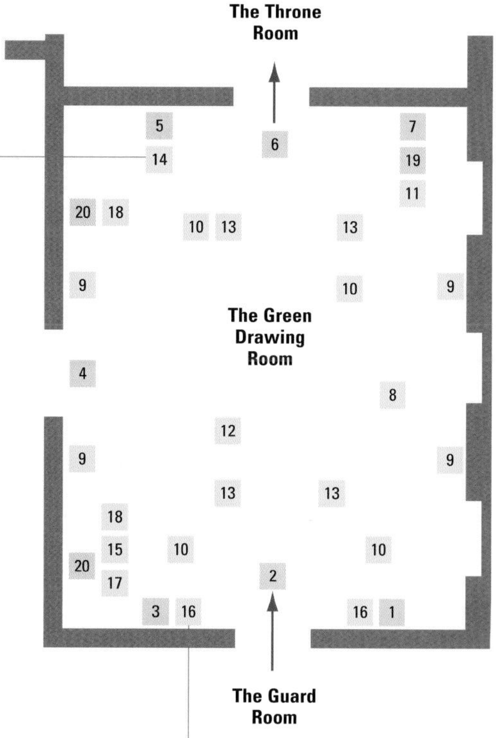

PICTURES

1 Allan Ramsay, *Queen Charlotte with her two eldest sons*, c.1764

2 German School, *Frederick Henry, Charles Louis and Elizabeth* (children of Frederick V and Elizabeth, King and Queen of Bohemia), 1618-19. Painted in Heidelberg, the painting was sent to the children's grandfather, James I.

3 Nathaniel Dance, *Edward Augustus, Duke of York* (brother of George III), 1764

4 John Michael Wright, *James, Duke of Cambridge* (son of James II and his first wife Anne Hyde), 1666–7

5 Angelica Kauffmann, *Augusta, Duchess of Brunswick, with her son, Charles, 1767.* (Augusta was the sister of George III and mother of Queen Caroline, consort of George IV.)

6 Attributed to Sofonisba Anguissola, *Isabella Clara Eugenia and Catharina* (daughters of Philip II, King of Spain), c.1569–70

7 Sir Martin Archer Shee, *Richard, Marquess Wellesley* (brother of the 1st Duke of Wellington, when Lord Steward of the Household), c.1832

FURNITURE

8 Grand piano with six-octave action by Isaac Mott, 1817; purchased by George IV in 1820 for £238 5s, it was originally placed in the Music Room Gallery at the Royal Pavilion, Brighton, together with the music stool.

9 Four semi-circular pedestals, gilded wood, c.1790; probably made in England to a French design for the Throne Room, Carlton House. The pedestals support gilt and patinated bronze French Empire candelabra.

10 Suite of seat furniture by Morel & Seddon, 1826–8; made for Windsor Castle.

11 Side table by Adam Weisweiler, veneered with ebony, c.1785. The panels of *pietra dura* (hardstone) probably date from the late 17th century. It was bought in Paris for George IV in 1816.

12 Regency centre table veneered in rosewood inlaid with brass.

13 Four early 19th-century cut-glass chandeliers.

14 Cabinet by Adam Weisweiler, veneered in ebony with Boulle marquetry, *pietra dura* panels and gilt-bronze mounts, c.1780–5.

15 Four-light candelabra by Benjamin Lewis Vulliamy, gilt and patinated bronze in the form of three female figures standing back to back, 1811; its design is inspired by the French Empire style.

16 Two Flemish (?) cabinets, c.1700, on later stands, veneered with tortoiseshell, pewter and ebony in *première-* and *contre-partie* marquetry (pewter on tortoiseshell and tortoiseshell on pewter).

17 French Empire clock with a figure of Apollo, probably designed by Martin-Eloi Lignereux with mounts supplied by Pierre-Philippe Thomire, 1803; bought by George IV in 1810.

18 Pair of Empire gilt and patinated bronze seven-light candelabra.

PORCELAIN

19 Minton bone china pot-pourri vase copying a Sèvres porcelain original, 1878.

20 Sèvres porcelain green ground vases, second half of the 18th century.

The Throne Room

THE THRONE ROOM was designed for investitures and ceremonial receptions of dignitaries, but in the early years of her reign it was also used by Queen Victoria as a ballroom. The Queen was very fond of music and dancing, and before the death of Prince Albert in 1861 held numerous concerts and balls at Buckingham Palace. Several of these occasions were *bals costumés*, such as the Stuart Ball held in the Throne Room in 1851, when all the guests dressed in the style of Charles II's court.

The Throne Room is now used principally for the reception of formal addresses on important occasions, such as those presented at The Queen's Jubilees in 1977 and 2002. Royal wedding photographs taken in this room include The Queen's own in 1947, and that of Lady Diana Spencer and The Prince of Wales in 1981.

Twenty metres (65 feet) long, the Throne Room is dominated by a baroque 'proscenium' arch, flanked by a pair of lively winged genii holding gilded garlands above the 'chairs of state'. The genii are Bernasconi's masterpiece. They hold free-hanging swags modelled completely in the round – a virtuoso artistic performance on Bernasconi's part – from which is suspended a medallion with the cypher of George IV.

Eugène Lami, *The Stuart Ball*, 1851

The wedding photograph of HRH Princess Elizabeth (now HM Queen Elizabeth II) and the Duke of Edinburgh, 20 November 1947.

The plaster frieze around the walls, which was designed by Thomas Stothard, is also remarkable for its attempt to treat a medieval subject – the Wars of the Roses – as if it were part of the Parthenon in Athens. It is only the Gothic armour that gives the game away. The subjects are the Battle of Tewkesbury (north), the marriage of Henry VII and Elizabeth of York (east), the Battle of Bosworth (west) and Bellona, goddess of war, encouraging the troops (south). The same attempt to assimilate medieval ideas in classical dress enlivens the bold display of heraldry of the four kingdoms of England, Scotland, Ireland and Hanover and the Garter Stars, on the plaster coving.

The elaborate door-case opposite the throne is of artificial stone (now painted) and was made by William Croggan; the little bust of William IV above it shows that the decoration of this room was completed to Nash's designs after George IV's death. The crimson silk hangings on the walls are a 20th-century restoration, but the four carved and gilt trophies on either side of the throne may have come from Carlton House.

Many of the other contents of the Throne Room also came from Carlton House, including the bronze and cut-glass chandeliers, the gilt-bronze candelabra on the chimneypiece and the giltwood and velvet benches flanking the door from the Green Drawing Room.

ABOVE: Detail of the 'proscenium' arch in the Throne Room.

RIGHT: The 'Oath of the Horatii' clock by Claude Galle, c.1800. Based on the famous painting by Jacques-Louis David of 1784, it was bought by George IV in 1809. It shows three brothers being given swords by their father after taking a vow to establish the supremacy of Rome.

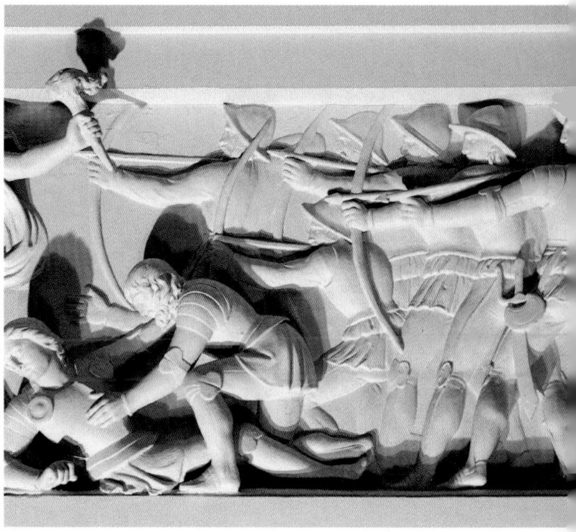

ABOVE: Detail of a group of archers from the 1828 plaster frieze of the Wars of the Roses in the Throne Room. The frieze was designed by Thomas Stothard and modelled by E. H. Baily.

FITTINGS

1 Four trophies of gilded wood, c.1795. Said to have come from the Throne Room, Carlton House.

FURNITURE

2 'Oath of the Horatii' clock by Claude Galle, c.1800.

3 Pair of candelabra attributed to Claude Galle, gilt and painted bronze in the form of cornucopias, early 19th century; purchased by George IV in 1814.

4 Throne chairs of HM The Queen and The Duke of Edinburgh by White, Allom & Co.; made for the Coronation ceremony of 1953.

5 Throne chairs of King George VI and Queen Elizabeth by White, Allom & Co.; made for the Coronation ceremony of 1937.

6 Throne chair of Queen Victoria by Thomas Dowbiggin, 1837.

7 Chandeliers, cut glass and gilt-bronze, c.1810; probably from Carlton House.

8 Pair of Regency giltwood and crimson velvet benches from the Ante-Throne Room at Carlton House.

PORCELAIN

9 Pair of Chinese porcelain jardinières, early 18th century; the gilt-bronze mounts attributed to Benjamin Lewis Vulliamy, c.1820.

SCULPTURE

10 Carlo Marochetti, *Prince Arthur*, c.1855

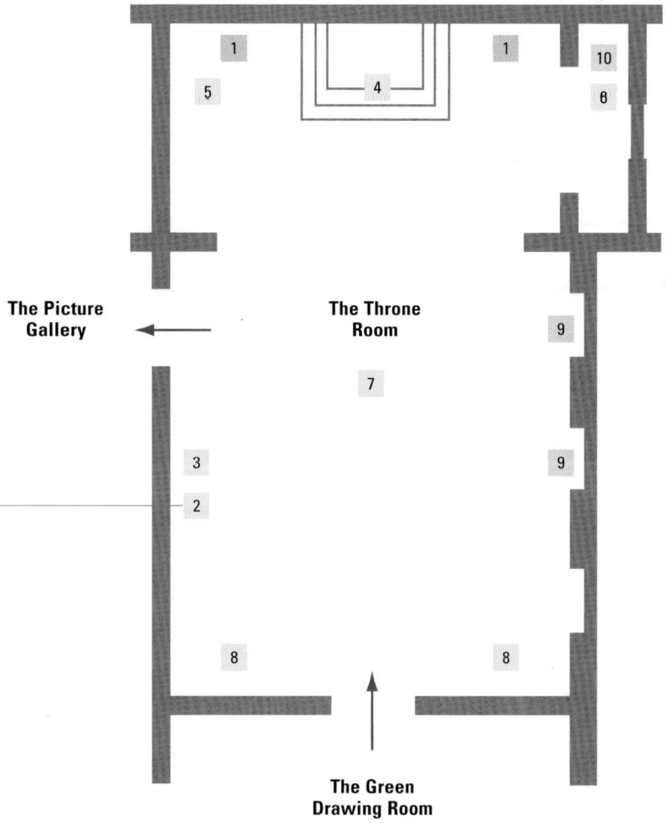

THE PICTURE GALLERY. The original glazed ceiling by John Nash, altered by Edward Blore, was replaced in 1914 to the designs of Frank Baines. The wall coverings have been changed several times since the Gallery was constructed by Nash.

The Picture Gallery

THE PICTURE GALLERY IS 50 METRES (155 FEET) LONG

IT WAS DESIGNED BY JOHN NASH FOR GEORGE IV

THE PAINTINGS HUNG HERE TODAY ARE PART OF ONE OF THE FINEST COLLECTIONS IN THE WORLD

THE PICTURE GALLERY at Buckingham Palace is the great spine of the state apartments. It occupies the site of the first-floor rooms of old Buckingham House, and was designed by Nash to display George IV's outstanding collection of Dutch and Flemish paintings, many of which still hang here. At Carlton House, paintings and sculpture had been scattered throughout the rooms, but for Buckingham Palace George IV planned a sculpture gallery and a picture gallery (one over the other) especially for the display of his finest works of art.

The original ceiling of the Picture Gallery was a complex design combining a timber hammerbeam frame with hanging pendants and a series of 17 little glazed saucer domes, or lanterns. It was something of a practical failure as it leaked and failed to throw light on the pictures. It was modified by Edward Blore, who was commissioned by the Government to finish the palace after George IV's death and Nash's dismissal (Blore had a reputation for being able to work within a budget), and totally remodelled for King George V in 1914 as a glazed segmental arched ceiling. At the same time the door cases were simplified and the columnar screen at the south end was redesigned. The architect for these changes was Frank Baines, chief architect of the Office of Works. The wood carvings, in the style of Grinling Gibbons, were made by H. H. Martyn of Cheltenham. The overall result is rather like the interior of the saloon of one of the great ocean liners of the period and it makes a striking contrast to the extreme opulence of Nash's adjoining rooms.

The four Carrara marble chimneypieces (again supplied by Joseph Browne), survive from the gallery's first incarnation and were designed by Nash. They each display a circular portrait-relief of a famous artist: Dürer, Rubens, Titian and Michelangelo.

In the mid-nineteenth century there was a total of 185 paintings in the gallery, but today what makes this part of the palace so remarkable is the quality, not the quantity, of the paintings hung here. They include works by Rubens, Rembrandt, Guercino, Canaletto, Claude Lorrain, Van Dyck and Guido Reni.

The Royal Collection today is one of the most extensive art collections in the world. It was begun by Charles I in the seventeenth century, and though his works of art, including his paintings, were dispersed during the Commonwealth (1649-59), several were later re-acquired, notably Van Dyck's magnificent equestrian portrait of the King with Monsieur de St Antoine, painted in 1633. The collection was considerably enriched in the eighteenth century by Frederick, Prince of Wales (the elder son of George II), and by George III. The largest group of paintings in the Picture Gallery today, however, is that assembled by George IV, some of which are illustrated on the following pages.

THE PICTURE GALLERY IN 1910, showing the arrangement of the pictures and the ceiling as altered by Edward Blore.

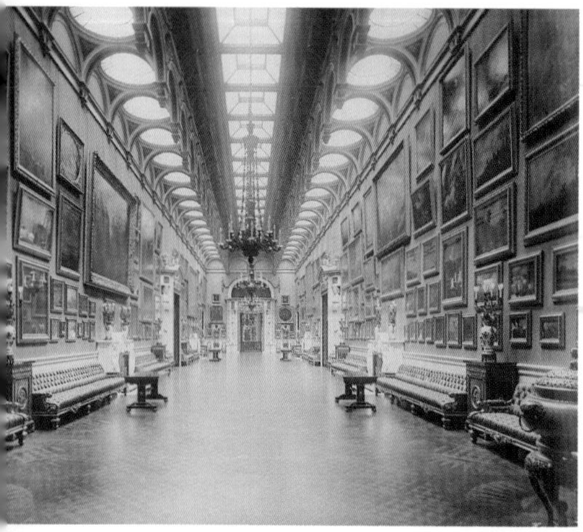

ABOVE: Douglas Morrison, *The Picture Gallery, Buckingham Palace*, 1843

RIGHT: THE PICTURE GALLERY prepared for a dinner given by The Prince of Wales to mark the eightieth birthday of the late Lord Menuhin, 1996.

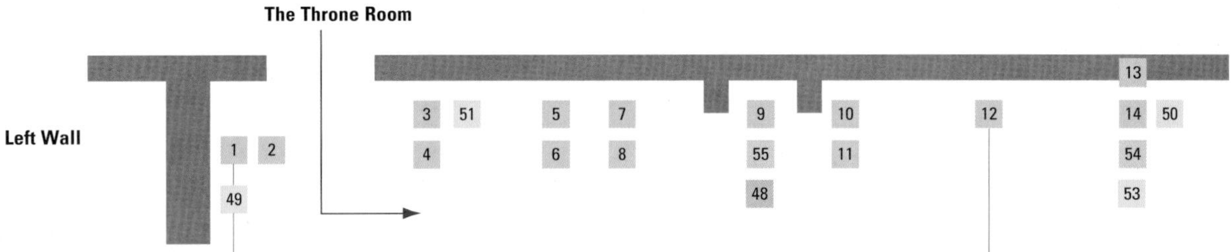

PICTURES (left wall)

PLEASE NOTE
The inventory numbers occasionally seen on the frames of paintings in the Picture Gallery should be ignored by visitors using the lists below.

1 Guercino, *The Libyan Sibyl*, c.1651

2 Barent Graat, *A family group*, 1658

3 David Teniers the Younger, *The Stolen Kiss*, c.1640

4 Jan Steen, *Interior of a tavern with cardplayers and a violin player*, c.1665

5 Sir Anthony Van Dyck, *Virgin and Child*, c.1630–32

6 Jan Both, *Landscape with St Philip baptising the eunuch*, c.1640

7 Nicholas Berchem, *A mountainous landscape with herdsmen driving cattle down a road*, 1673

8 Rembrandt van Rijn, *Christ and Mary Magdalen at the tomb*, 1638

9 Francesco Zuccarelli, *Landscape with two young children offering fruit to a woman*, c.1743

10 David Teniers the Younger, *Fishermen on the seashore*, c.1660

11 Sir Anthony Van Dyck, *Zeger van Hontsum*, c.1630

12 Rembrandt van Rijn, *The Shipbuilder and his wife*, c.1633

13 Aelbert Cuyp, *Cows in a pasture beside a river before the ruins of the abbey of Rijnsburg*, 1640–50

14 Hendrick ter Bruggen, *A laughing bravo with a bass viol and a glass*, 1625

15 Sir Anthony Van Dyck, *Charles I and Henrietta Maria with their two eldest children ('The Greate Peece')*, 1632

16 Antonio Canaletto, *Venice: The Piazzetta towards the Torre dell'Orologio*, c.1728

17 Luca Carlevaris, *A caprice landscape with a fountain and an artist sketching*, c.1710

1: Guercino, *The Libyan Sibyl*, c.1651

12: Rembrandt van Rijn, *The Shipbuilder and his wife*, c.1633

15: Sir Anthony Van Dyck, *Charles I and Henrietta Maria with their two eldest children ('The Greate Peece')*, 1632

18 Gaspar Dughet, *Seascape with Jonah and the whale*, c.1653

19 Melchior de Hondecoeter, *Birds and a spaniel*, c.1665

20 Sir Peter Paul Rubens, *Landscape with St George and the dragon*, c.1630

21 Luca Carlevaris, *A caprice view of a seaport*, c.1710

22 Claude Lorrain, *The Rape of Europa*, 1667

FITTINGS

48 Chimneypieces supplied by Joseph Browne and carved by Italian sculptors, late 1820s; incorporating profile busts of Titian, Rubens, Dürer and Michelangelo.

FURNITURE

49 Pair of cabinets by Pierre Garnier, veneered with ebony and inlaid with panels of pewter, tortoiseshell and brass, c.1770; bought for George IV in Paris in 1819.

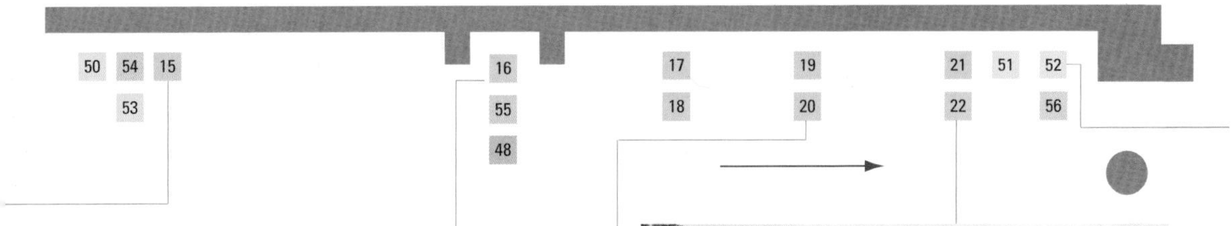

22: Claude Lorrain, *The Rape of Europa*, 1667

52: One of two pedestals by Gilles Joubert supporting an 18th-century bronze bust of the Emperor Augustus.

16: Antonio Canaletto, *Venice: The Piazzetta towards the Torre dell'Orologio*, c.1728

20: Peter Paul Rubens, *Landscape with St George and the dragon*, c.1630

50 Four armchairs by Georges Jacob, c.1786; imported into England by Dominique Daguerre in the late 1780s. Originally placed in the Prince's bedroom at Carlton House.

51 Set of four French console tables attributed to Adam Weisweiler, marble-topped and veneered with tulipwood, c.1785. The gilt-bronze scrollwork was added by Benjamin Lewis Vulliamy in 1811.

52 Two pedestals supplied by Gilles Joubert, veneered with trellis marquetry in kingwood and tulipwood, 1762. Made to support clocks giving solar and lunar time, they originally stood on either side of the alcove in Louis XV's bedroom at Versailles. They now support 18th-century bronze busts of the Emperors Augustus and Vespasian. Acquired by George IV in 1818.

53 Two pairs of Boulle cabinets in brass and pewter with gilt-bronze figurative plaques and friezes, acquired in 1828.

PORCELAIN AND LACQUER

54 Japanese lacquer bowls with French gilt-bronze mounts in the Louis XV and Louis XVI styles, 18th century.

55 Two pairs of hard-paste Sèvres porcelain vases, painted in platinum and gold on a black ground with chinoiserie scenes and with gilt-bronze mounts, c.1790–92; and another pair, with an undecorated black ground and siren mounts, c.1786.

56 Pair of large celadon vases in the form of ewers with French gilt-bronze mounts, early 19th century.

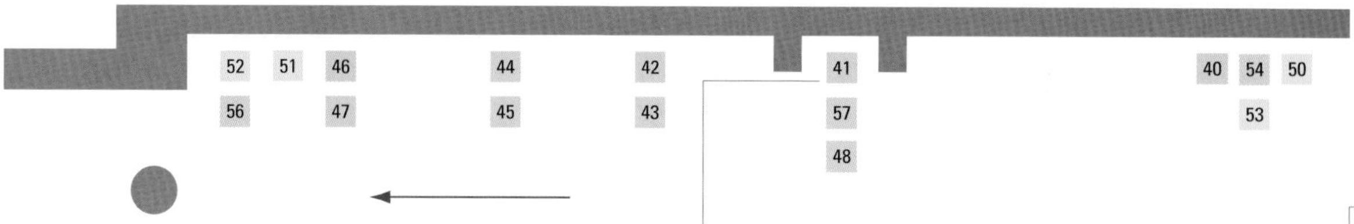

PICTURES (right wall)

23 Guido Reni, *The Death of Cleopatra*, c.1628

24 Gonzales Coques, *The family of Jan-Baptista Anthoine*, 1664

25 Nicolaes Maes, *The Listening Housewife*, 1655

26 Gabriel Metsu, *The Cello Player*, c.1665

27 Philips Wouwermans, *The Hayfield*, c.1660

28 Sir Peter Paul Rubens, *The Assumption of the Virgin*, c.1611

29 Sir Anthony Van Dyck, *The Mystic Marriage of St Catherine*, c.1630

30 David Teniers the Younger, *Peasants dancing outside a country house*, 1645

31 Philips Wouwermans, *A horse fair in front of a town*, c.1660

32 Pieter de Hooch, *A courtyard in Delft at evening: a woman spinning*, c.1656

33 Francesco Zuccarelli, *Landscape with two seated women embracing*, c.1743

34 Domenico Fetti, *Vincenzo Avogadro*, c.1620

35 Willem van de Velde the Younger, *A calm: a States yacht under sail, close to the shore, and many other vessels*, c.1655

36 Sir Anthony Van Dyck, *Christ healing the paralytic*, c.1619

37 Philips Wouwermans, *A cavalry skirmish*, c.1646

38 Carlo Dolci, *Salome with the head of St John the Baptist*, 1670

39 Willem van de Velde the Younger, *'The Golden Leeuw' at sea in heavy weather*, c.1671

40 Sir Peter Paul Rubens and studio, *The family of Sir Balthasar Gerbier*, c.1629–39

41 Antonio Canaletto, *Venice: Piazza S. Marco from a corner of the Basilica*, 1728

42 Luca Carlevaris, *A caprice view with a shipyard*, c.1710

43 Gaspard Dughet, *Landscape with a waterfall*, 1653–4

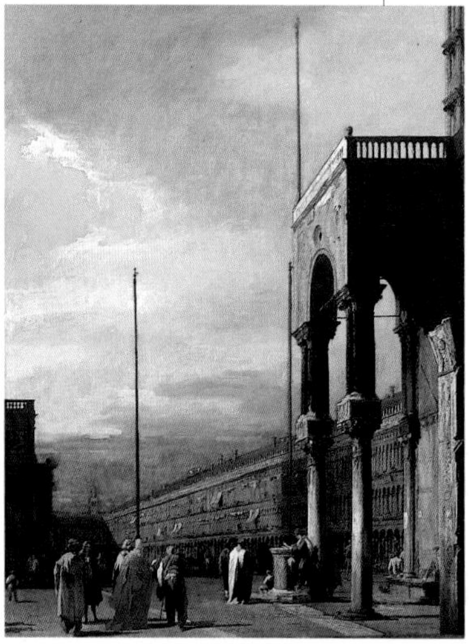

41: Antonio Canaletto, *Venice: Piazza S. Marco from a corner of the Basilica*, 1728

32: Pieter de Hooch, *A courtyard in Delft at evening: a woman spinning*, c.1656

35: Willem van de Velde the Younger, *A calm: a States yacht under sail, close to the shore, and many other vessels*, c.1655

44 Jan Steen, *A village revel*, c.1673

45 Aelbert Cuyp, *Landscape with a negro page*, c.1655

46 Luca Carlevaris, *A caprice view of a harbour*, c.1710

47 Gaspard Dughet, *Landscape with figures by a pool*, c.1665

Key to Fittings and Furniture 48-56 is given under the room plan for the left wall of the Picture Gallery on pp.42-43.

PORCELAIN AND LACQUER

57 Pair of *lac burgauté* (black lacquer with mother-of-pearl inlay) vases, with gilt-bronze mounts by the Vulliamys, early 19th century.

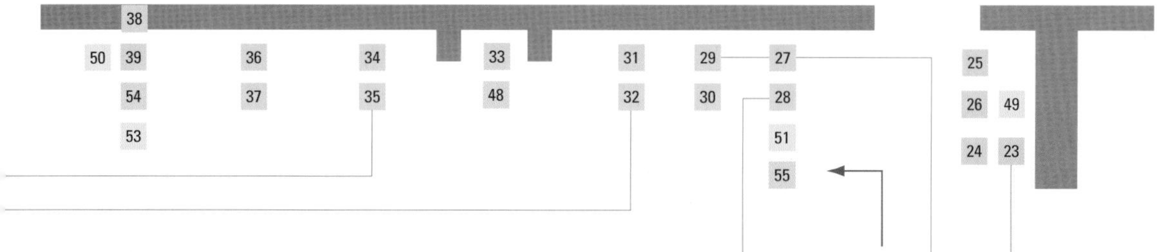

23: Guido Reni, *The Death of Cleopatra*, c.1628

29: Sir Anthony Van Dyck, *The Mystic Marriage of St Catherine*, c.1630

28: Sir Peter Paul Rubens, *The Assumption of the Virgin*, c.1611

The Picture Gallery Lobby

Sir Francis Chantrey, *Mrs Jordan and two of her children*, 1834

THE PICTURE GALLERY LOBBY is divided from the main part of the gallery by a screen of white marble Corinthian columns, but is otherwise treated in the same architectural manner, with a door case by Martyn of Cheltenham and a plaster frieze of 1914 by Frank Baines. The most interesting object here is the life-size marble statue by Sir Francis Chantrey of Mrs Jordan and two of her children. Mrs Jordan was a celebrated actress (in the East Gallery there is a portrait of her as the Comic Muse; see page 48), and the mistress of the Duke of Clarence, later William IV, before his marriage to Princess Adelaide of Saxe-Meiningen and his succession to the throne. Her five sons and five daughters by the Duke took the name Fitzclarence, with the eldest son, George Augustus Frederick, being created Earl of Munster in 1831. This charming statue was commissioned by William IV in 1834, eighteen years after Mrs Jordan's death, and was bequeathed to The Queen in 1975 by the 5th Earl of Munster.

Hanging behind the statue is one of George IV's more unusual acquisitions, a large panel of embroidered silk depicting *The Annunciation.* It dates from the mid-seventeenth century and was originally made for an Italian church, where such panels were hung on great feast days.

Sir Martin Archer Shee, *William IV*, 1833

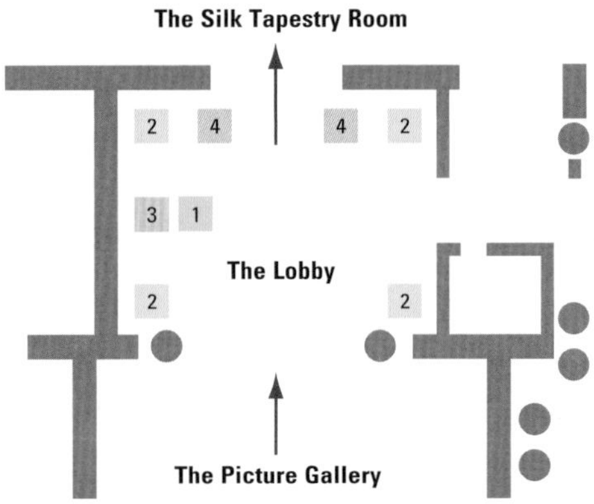

SCULPTURE

1 Sir Francis Chantrey, *Mrs Jordan and two of her children*, 1834

FURNITURE

2 Set of lyre-backed chairs, part gilded, probably made for Carlton House by François Hervé, c.1790.

EMBROIDERY

3 Large Italian needlework panel of *The Annunciation* within an arabesque border, mid-17th century.

PORCELAIN

4 Pair of large octagonal Chinese porcelain vases, late 18th century.

The Silk Tapestry Room

Sir George Hayter, *Queen Victoria*, 1840

THE SILK TAPESTRY ROOM was contrived by Blore as a link between the Grand Staircase, the Picture Gallery and the garden-front state rooms. It takes its name from the Italian needlework panels which formerly hung in this area.

The two paintings by Sir George Hayter now hanging in this room date from the beginning of Queen Victoria's reign. His state portrait depicts the young Queen in Coronation robes (Hayter's representation of the actual Coronation can be seen next door in the East Gallery). Queen Victoria's eldest son, the future King Edward VII, was born on 9 November 1841, and his christening in St George's Chapel, Windsor, is also portrayed here by Hayter.

The monumental French pedestal clock with Rococo ormolu decoration was another of George IV's acquisitions for Carlton House, where it formed a focal point on the principal staircase.

PICTURES

1 Sir George Hayter, *The Christening of The Prince of Wales, 25 January 1842*, 1842–5

2 Sir George Hayter, *Queen Victoria*, 1840

3 Benjamin Robert Haydon, *The Mock Election*, 1827

FURNITURE

4 Chest of drawers by Adam Weisweiler, with mahogany veneer, late 18th century

5 Table by Morel & Seddon, ebony with a *pietra dura* slab and gilt-bronze mounts, raised on four pairs of gilded wood supports, c.1828; made for Windsor Castle.

6 Giltwood side table with specimen marble top, attributed to Mayhew & Ince, c.1775. Purchased by Queen Mary in 1931.

7 French clock by François-Louis Godon, white marble and gilt-bronze, carved with figures of Venus and Cupid, 1792.

8 Monumental pedestal clock, veneered with tulipwood and fitted with elaborately chased gilt and patinated bronze mounts. It was probably made in the 1730s, possibly by Jean-Pierre Latz, and was bought by George IV in 1816. The later English movement is by Vulliamy.

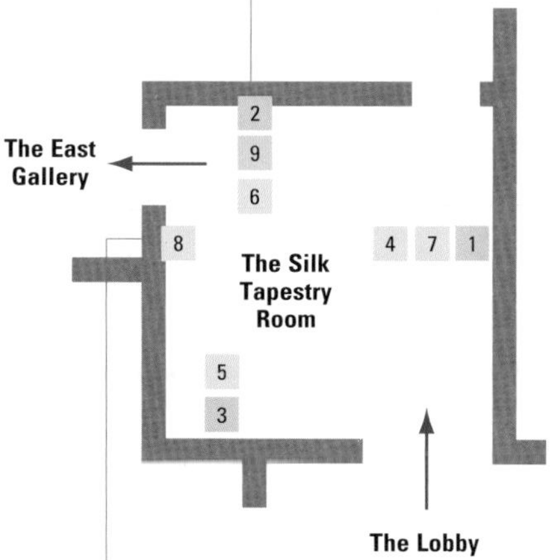

SCULPTURE

9 Small bronze copy of the equestrian statue of Louis XV after Edmé Bouchardon which was unveiled in 1763 in the Place Louis XV (now Place de la Concorde), Paris; this reduction is one of seven cast by Louis-Claude Vassé, c.1764.

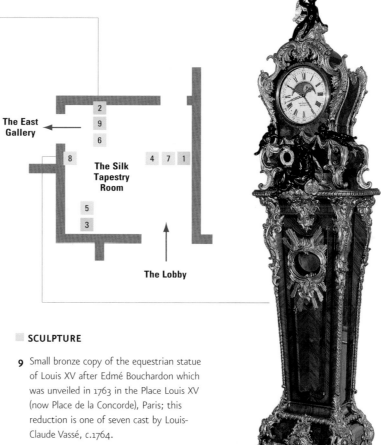

Monumental pedestal clock from the Silk Tapestry Room.

The East Gallery

John Hoppner, *Mrs Jordan as the Comic Muse*, 1786

THE EAST GALLERY is part of the new block of rooms added to the south end of the west range of the palace in 1853–5 by Queen Victoria and Prince Albert. They provided a vast new ballroom and a series of galleries for royal processions. Designed by James Pennethorne, Nash's pupil and protégé at the Office of Works, the new rooms were built by Thomas Cubitt. Their interior finishing and decoration was executed under the immediate direction of the Prince Consort and a team of artists whom he admired. These included Professor Ludwig Gruner from Dresden and the artist Nicolà Consoni from Rome, where the latter had been responsible for some of the paintings in the basilica of San Paolo Fuori le Mura. Much of Consoni's decoration at the palace was covered up in the course of various redecorations in the last century, but his gold and grisaille panels of cupids at play still survive here.

The East Gallery extends southwards towards the Ballroom from the Grand Staircase and contains another of the marble chimneypieces designed by Nash and made under Joseph Browne's direction at Carrara in the 1820s, *en suite* with those in the Picture Gallery. This one features a carved portrait roundel of Rembrandt.

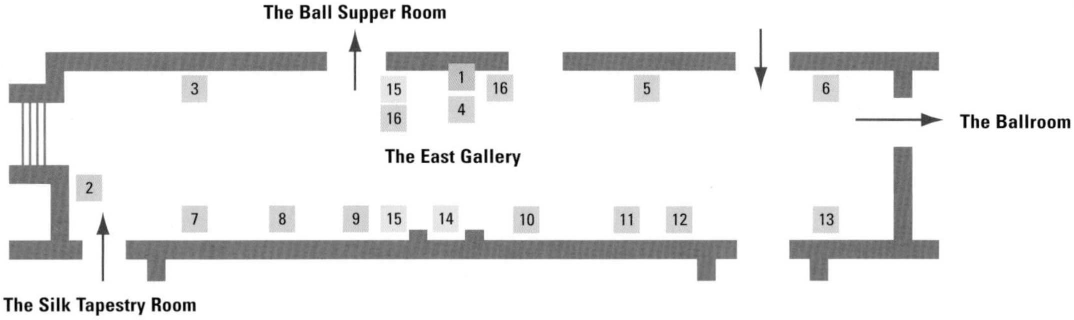

FITTINGS

1 Chimneypiece supplied by Joseph Browne, late 1820s, incorporating a profile bust of Rembrandt.

PICTURES

2 John Hoppner, *Mrs Jordan as the Comic Muse*, 1786

3 Heinrich Hansen, *Christiansborg Palace from Højbro Plads, Copenhagen*, 1863

4 John Russell, *George, Prince of Wales* (later George IV), 1791; the Prince is in the uniform of the Royal Kentish Bowmen.

5 Franz Xaver Winterhalter, *The Royal Family in 1846*

6 Benjamin West, *The Apotheosis of Prince Octavius*, 1783

7 Benjamin West, *Queen Charlotte*, 1782

8 Benjamin West, *Prince Adolphus (later Duke of Cambridge), with Princesses Mary and Sophia*, 1778

9 Benjamin West, *George III*, 1779

10 John Hoppner, *Francis, 5th Duke of Bedford*, c.1797

11 Sir George Hayter, *The Coronation of Queen Victoria*, 1838

12 John Hoppner, *Francis, 5th Earl of Moira and 1st Marquess of Hastings*, c.1793

13 Sir Thomas Lawrence, *Caroline, Princess of Wales, and Princess Charlotte*, 1802

FURNITURE

14 Large clock signed by the Parisian bronze manufacturer De La Croix, gilt and patinated bronze, c.1775; the dial is a later insertion by Vulliamy. The pedestal incorporates four gilt-bronze plaques of 16th-century design.

15 Two pairs of candelabra by Pierre-Philippe Thomire, gilt-bronze supported by figures of patinated bronze, c.1810. The candelabra entered the collection in 1813. They stand on ebony and brass pedestals, French, early 19th century.

PORCELAIN

16 Pair of Sèvres porcelain vases with gilt-bronze mounts, c.1791-2.

ABOVE: The East Gallery.

RIGHT: Sir George Hayter, *The Coronation of Queen Victoria*, 1838

THE BALL SUPPER ROOM

TOGETHER, THE BALL SUPPER ROOM AND THE BALLROOM CAN ACCOMMODATE UP TO 600 GUESTS

BOTH ROOMS WERE CREATED AT THE INSTIGATION OF QUEEN VICTORIA, AND COMPLETED IN 1855

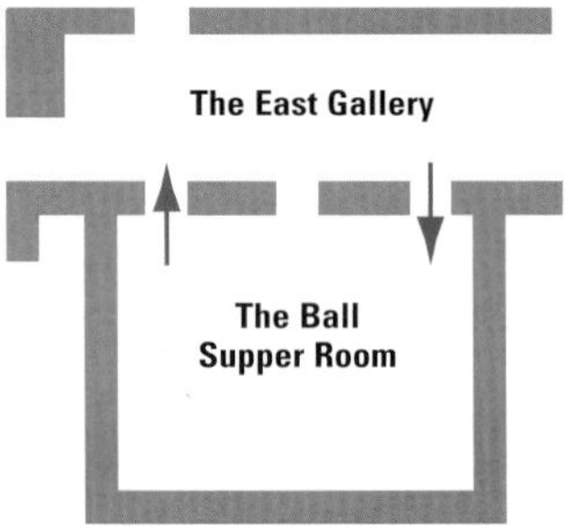

ON HER VISITS to foreign heads of state, Queen Victoria was entertained in some of the most splendid and spacious rooms of Europe, and in 1845 she wrote to the Prime Minister Sir Robert Peel of the 'urgent necessity' of providing rooms of equivalent capacity and status at Buckingham Palace. The Ballroom and the Ball Supper Room, both 14 metres (46 feet) high, were completed in 1855 to the designs of Sir James Pennethorne.

The interiors of both rooms were originally elaborately decorated in bright colours borrowed from Italian Renaissance palace interiors by Prince Albert's adviser on decoration, Ludwig Gruner. In this respect they have parallels in the contemporary interiors of Leo von Klenze, designed for Tsar Nicholas I at the Hermitage in St Petersburg.

The three pairs of doors to the Supper Room are surmounted by paired plaster groups designed by John Gibson and modelled by William Theed, representing Mercury, Bacchus and Apollo, and by two water nymphs. One of the marble chimneypieces, incorporating small busts of George IV and William IV, was re-used from the Armoury which formerly occupied this part of the palace; the other, which has busts of Queen Victoria and Prince Albert, was made to match it.

The Ball Supper Room, with tables laid, c.1920-30.

THE BALLROOM

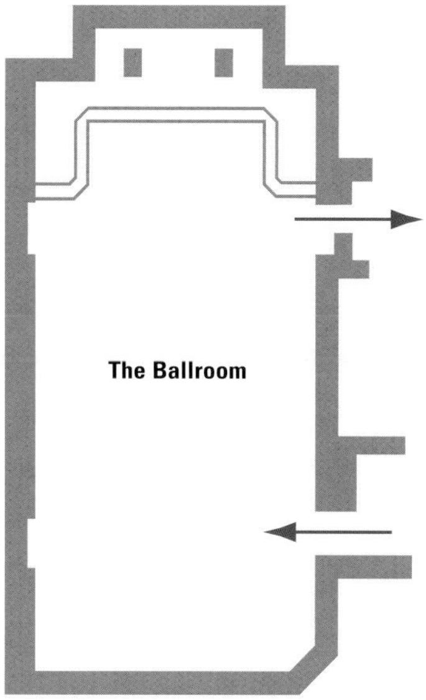

THIS ENORMOUS ROOM, 14 metres high, 34 metres long and 18 wide (46 x 111 x 59 feet) was first used for a ball on 8 May 1856. Designed from the start as a ball- and concert room, it also formed the setting for grand orchestral concerts throughout the rest of Queen Victoria's reign and into the early twentieth century. The performers were invariably Queen Victoria's private band, supplemented by choral singers from the opera houses and celebrated soloists such as Adelina Patti, and the programmes would include music by Rossini, the Strauss family, Beethoven and Handel. Perhaps the Queen and Prince Albert's favourite of all composers was Felix Mendelssohn (1809-47), who played for them at Buckingham Palace on three occasions. The Strauss orchestra was another favourite; the Alice Polka, named after Queen Victoria's daughter Princess Alice, was first performed at a ball held in the palace in 1849.

The organ in the Ballroom was originally supplied in 1817 by Henry Cephas Lincoln for the Music Room at Brighton Pavilion. It was moved here after Queen Victoria sold the Pavilion to Brighton Corporation in 1848 and had the contents brought to London for incorporation in Buckingham Palace. The organ was rebuilt and extended by Gray and Davison and installed in a new case

Louis Haghe, *The New Ballroom*, 1856. The Ballroom's original brightly coloured decoration, designed by Ludwig Gruner, can be seen in this watercolour.

designed by Gruner, flanked by plaster figures by William Theed the Younger, symbolising Music, and ornamented with two gilded roundels of the composer G.F. Handel. After an extensive restoration lasting five years, the organ is now in playing condition for the first time in almost a century.

Further plaster statues by Theed stand on top of the arch at the opposite end of the room, sheltering the throne and flanking a double medallion of Queen Victoria and Prince Albert in profile, held up by seated figures symbolising History and Fame. The canopy is an adaptation of the Imperial *shamiana* made to the designs of Sir Edwin Lutyens for King George V and Queen Mary's thrones at the Delhi Durbar of 1911.

Today the Ballroom is regularly used for investitures, at which recipients of honours receive their insignia from The Queen. These insignia, as well as the sword with which The Queen confers knighthoods, are displayed in the cases around the room. The Ballroom also forms the setting for the state banquets given by The Queen in honour of visiting heads of state.

The two thrones in the Ballroom were made by Carlhian & Baumetz under the direction of the famous art adviser Joseph Duveen for the use of King Edward VII and Queen Alexandra at the Coronation of 1902. The gilt-bronze torchères are from a set of ten supplied for the room by the Paris firm of Barbedienne in 1856. The Ballroom also contains two tapestries from a set woven at the Gobelins factory in Paris in 1776 and illustrating the story of Jason and the Golden Fleece.

ABOVE: Elizabeth Taylor being invested with the insignia of Dame Commander of the Order of the British Empire in 2000.

LEFT: The Ballroom at Buckingham Palace arranged for a state banquet.

THE WEST GALLERY

THE WEST GALLERY, smaller than the East Gallery, was also designed by Pennethorne and decorated originally by Ludwig Gruner, under Prince Albert's direction.

The arched tympana above the doors at either end of the gallery have spirited plaster sculptures in the style of those in George IV's rooms. They are the work of William Theed the Younger, a sculptor who was admired by Prince Albert and who also worked at the Royal Mews. Prince Albert's aim was to introduce a serious 'artistic' note into the decoration of the palace, drawing on the High Renaissance style that he and Gruner were keen to promote in England. The style is similar to that favoured by other German princely patrons of the mid-nineteenth century, for example in the royal residences at Potsdam, Dresden and Munich.

In the West Gallery are four Gobelins tapestries from the *Don Quixote* series which were given to George IV in 1789 by the artist Richard Cosway, one of the circle of friends and advisers to the Prince known as the 'Carlton House set'. (Cosway himself had been given them, while in Paris two years earlier, by Louis XVI.) Cosway was one of the Prince's chief artistic advisers in the 1780s and helped to influence George IV's taste for French fashion and art, with results that are spectacularly represented at Buckingham Palace.

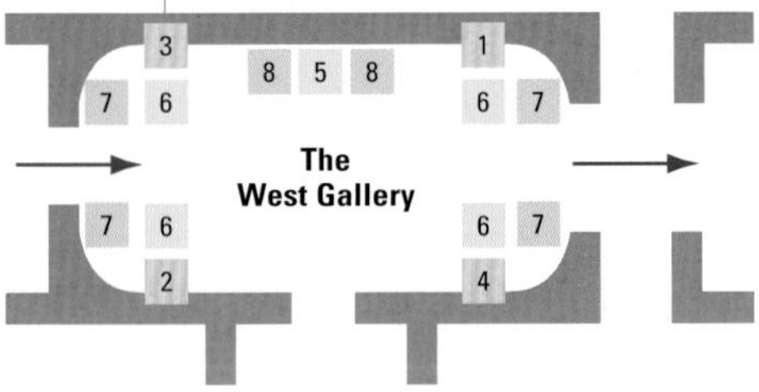

THE WEST GALLERY

TAPESTRIES

Four tapestries from a series of 28 illustrating the exploits of Don Quixote, woven at the Gobelins manufactory, second half of the 18th century.

1 The false Princess Micomicon beseeches Don Quixote to restore her to the throne

2 Don Quixote cured by wisdom of his folly

3 Sancho Panza despairs at the loss of his donkey

4 Sancho Panza's memorable judgement

FURNITURE

5 Boulle knee-hole desk, veneered with tortoiseshell, ebony and brass, late 17th century.

6 Giltwood chairs designed by Robert Jones and made by Tatham, Bailey & Sanders for the Royal Pavilion, Brighton, 1823.

PORCELAIN

7 Four Chinese porcelain vases on marble pedestals with mounts by the Vulliamys, 1808–14.

8 Two Chinese Imari-pattern square baluster vases and covers, c.1750.

ABOVE: Detail of the plaster sculpture by William Theed in the West Gallery. It depicts Thetis bearing the armour of Achilles.

LEFT: *Sancho Panza despairs at the loss of his donkey*; one of four Gobelins tapestries from a series of twenty-eight illustrating the exploits of Don Quixote, second half of the 18th century. The tapestries were given to George IV by the artist Richard Cosway.

The State Dining Room

THE STATE DINING ROOM IS USED REGULARLY BY THE QUEEN FOR OFFICIAL ENTERTAINING

THE DECORATION OF THE ROOM SPANNED THE REIGN OF WILLIAM IV AND CONTINUED INTO THAT OF QUEEN VICTORIA. BOTH OF THEIR CYPHERS CAN BE SEEN IN THE PLASTER ROUNDELS ON THE WALLS

THE STATE DINING ROOM was originally intended to be a music room; the pair of white marble chimneypieces, possibly the work of Matthew Cotes Wyatt, show flanking female figures playing musical instruments. The Nash-like ceiling, with its three little saucer domes, appears more refined than the coving, with its heavy and relentless brackets.

The rebuilding of this room as a dining room was one of William IV's few alterations to his predecessors' layout of the state rooms. The new King wanted a dining room on the principal floor adjoining the drawing rooms, rather than on the ground floor as Nash and George IV had envisaged. The character of the room is largely due to Edward Blore, as the pier glasses, pelmets and other florid gilded enrichments of the room were all designed by him.

The principal feature of the room is the series of splendid, full-length state portraits of some of the Hanoverian sovereigns of Britain, in gilded frames supplied by Ponsonby & Sons in 1840. The alcove at the south end, which now contains the entrance to the West Gallery, was originally the sideboard recess, used for displaying gold plate during banquets, but it was altered when Pennethorne's wing was added in 1853–5.

A feature of the State Dining Room, and of all the rooms on the west side of the palace, is the beautiful view over the gardens, landscaped in the 1820s for George IV by Nash and William Townsend Aiton, the head gardener at Kew. The lake, the picturesque, naturalistic planting of trees and shrubs and the green lawns give the palace the feel of the country in the town.

Dining Silver at Buckingham Palace

The State Dining Room is used regularly by The Queen for official entertaining, luncheons and formal dinners. On these occasions the tables are set with part of the great collection of silver-gilt acquired over many years by George IV, mainly from the Crown goldsmiths Rundell, Bridge & Rundell. Some examples are displayed in this room, including the pair of ewers and stands made for the King in 1822 and an oval tureen by Paul Storr. George IV had a particular love of gold plate, and commissioned some of the most magnificent pieces ever made in England.

LEFT: One of a pair of silver-gilt ewers and stands by Rundell, Bridge & Rundell, 1822

THE STATE DINING ROOM, photographed in 1914.

The 'Apollo' clock, by Pierre-Philippe Thomire, gilt-bronze and marble, early 19th century. Bought by George IV in 1810, it shows Apollo in his chariot drawn by four horses. Its movement was replaced by Benjamin Lewis Vulliamy in 1834.

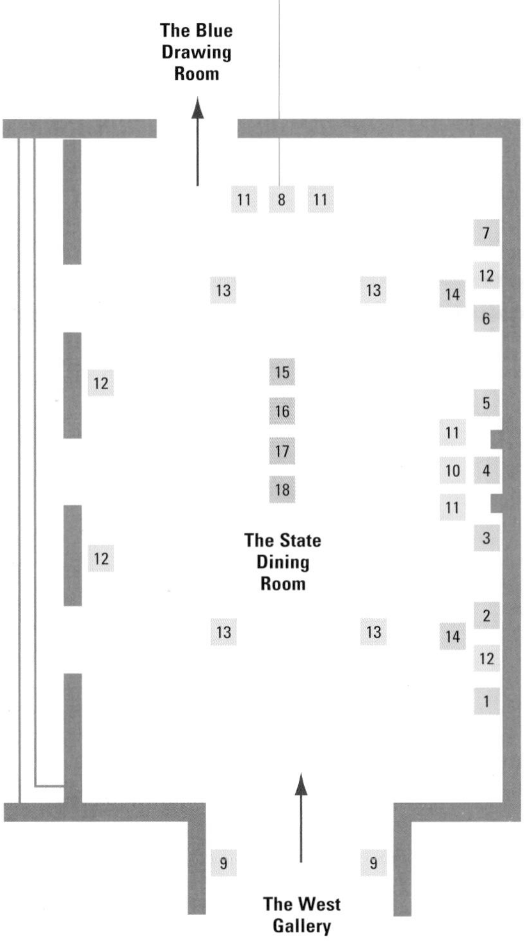

PICTURES

The display illustrates the development of state portraiture during the second half of the 18th century.

1 Sir Godfrey Kneller, *Caroline, Princess of Wales* (later Queen, wife of George II), 1716

2 Jean-Baptiste van Loo, *Frederick, Prince of Wales*, 1742

3 Allan Ramsay, *Queen Charlotte* (wife of George III), c.1763

4 Studio of Sir Thomas Lawrence, *King George IV in Garter Robes*, c.1820

5 Studio of Allan Ramsay, *George III*, c.1763

6 Jean-Baptiste van Loo, *Augusta, Princess of Wales* (wife of Frederick, Prince of Wales), 1742

7 Studio of John Shackleton, *George II*, 1755–7

FURNITURE

8 'Apollo' clock by Pierre-Philippe Thomire, early 19th century.

9 Pair of candelabra by Thomire & Cie, malachite and gilt-bronze, c.1828, on Regency giltwood tripods carved with griffins.

10 Clock by Benjamin Lewis Vulliamy, marble and gilt-bronze, fitted with three porcelain figures by William Duesbury of Derby, 1788; designed for the Prince of Wales (later George IV).

11 Set of four five-light candelabra by François Rémond, gilt-bronze on red marble bases, 1783. They were made for the *cabinet turc* of the comte d'Artois in his apartment at Versailles. The maize motif in the centre was thought at the time to be Turkish. Bought by George IV in 1820.

12 Set of parcel-gilt mahogany sideboards with gilt-bronze and mirrored glass backs, 1838.

13 Four early 19th-century English cut-glass and gilt-bronze chandeliers.

PORCELAIN

14 Chinese celadon porcelain vases with French and English gilt-bronze mounts, 18th and early 19th century; most of these were at the Royal Pavilion, Brighton, in the early 19th century.

DINING SILVER

15 Oval tureen, cover and stand by Paul Storr, silver gilt, 1818; made for Adolphus Frederick, Duke of Cambridge, younger brother of George IV.

16 Pair of wine bottle coolers by Digby Scott and Benjamin Smith, silver gilt, 1803; made for George IV.

17 Pair of ewers and stands by Rundell, Bridge & Rundell, silver gilt, 1822; made for George IV.

18 Centrepiece modelled by Edmund Cotterill for Garrards, 1842, to the designs of Prince Albert. It includes portraits of Queen Victoria's favourite dogs.

THE BLUE DRAWING ROOM

THE BLUE DRAWING ROOM is one of the finest rooms in the palace and the *ne plus ultra* of Georgian sumptuousness in decoration, even more splendid than the Throne Room sequence on the east front. George IV intended this room as a ballroom, but it was superseded in that function by Queen Victoria's Ballroom in the south-west wing. Today guests gather here for drinks before large luncheon parties and grand state and diplomatic occasions. It is 21 metres (68 feet) long and divided into bays by giant Corinthian columns.

The room was first known as the South Drawing Room, and its original decoration was a symphony of red, with porphyry scagliola columns, crimson velvet curtains and figured-silk wall hangings. The blue flock paper now in the room was hung by Queen Mary in the early twentieth century, while the Corinthian columns were re-painted to resemble onyx (and to cover up defects in the scagliola) in the reign of Queen Victoria.

The three moulded plaster reliefs in the tympana were modelled by William Pitts in 1835 and have a literary theme, depicting the apotheoses of Shakespeare (north), of Spenser (south) and of Milton (facing north).

LEFT: THE BLUE DRAWING ROOM. The ceiling, with its great billowing coves and bold console brackets, shows Nash at his most daring and original.

BELOW LEFT: Sir Luke Fildes, *State Portrait of King George V*, 1911–12

BELOW RIGHT: Sir William Llewellyn, *State Portrait of Queen Mary*, 1911–13

The Table of the Grand Commanders

The Blue Drawing Room contains one of George IV's favourite possessions – the Table of the Grand Commanders. The top of the table is of Sèvres porcelain, painted by Louis-Bertin Parant in *trompe-l'oeil* to resemble sardonyx cameos, with the head of Alexander the Great surrounded by similar portrait-heads of twelve other great commanders of antiquity. The ormolu mounts are by the famous metalworker Pierre-Philippe Thomire. The table was commissioned by Napoleon in 1806 when, as the conqueror of all Europe and the recently crowned Emperor of the French, he was at his apogee and saw himself as a modern Alexander the Great. It was presented by Louis XVIII of France to George IV, when still Prince Regent, in 1817. George IV was so thrilled by this magnificent trophy that he instructed the painter Sir Thomas Lawrence to include it in his State Portrait (see page 14). It was placed in the Bow Drawing Room at Carlton House before being brought here.

William Pitts (1790–1840) designed and modelled most of the high-relief plasterwork in the state rooms. He started life as a silver chaser and modeller and executed the famous silver-gilt Achilles Shield of 1821 to Flaxman's design. His work at Buckingham Palace has considerable grace and charm but is perhaps too small in scale to be appreciated in its lofty situation. Further examples of his work can be seen in the Music Room (page 65) and the White Drawing Room (page 66).

The Blue Drawing Room and the two rooms that follow are highlights among the interiors of Buckingham Palace. The richness of their fixtures and fittings distinguishes them from any comparable state rooms in England, and the originality of their architecture equally marks them out from contemporary palace rooms on the Continent. The aim of George IV and Nash, in which they triumphantly succeeded, was to create an aura of extreme opulence.

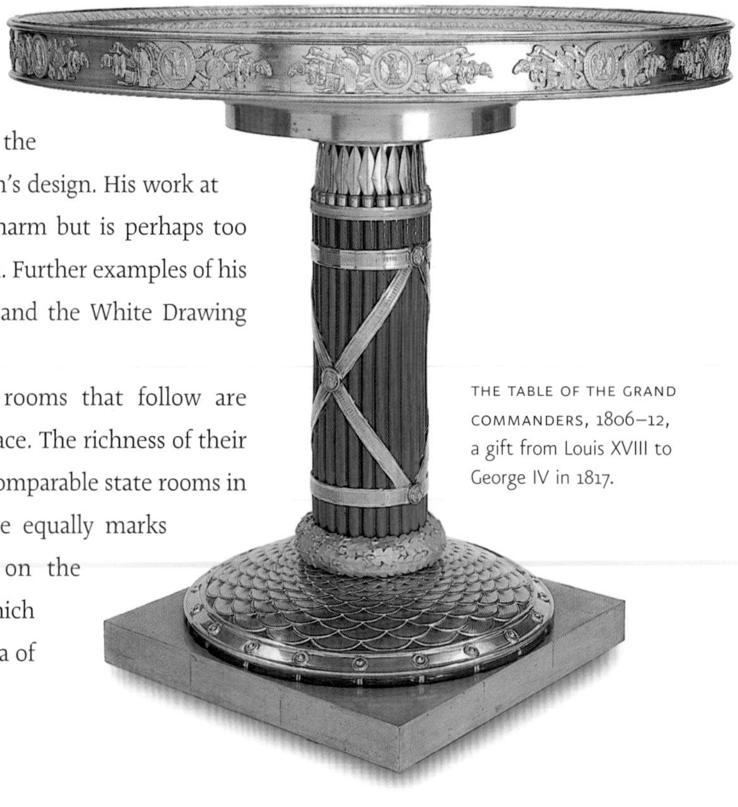

THE TABLE OF THE GRAND COMMANDERS, 1806–12, a gift from Louis XVIII to George IV in 1817.

The architecture of the Blue Drawing Room was the only part completed by George IV's death. Its decoration and furnishing were carried out in the reign of William IV under the supervision of Viscount Duncannon. The gilt sofas and some of the armchairs were made for Carlton House in the early part of the nineteenth century; while the four marble side tables with gilt-bronze mounts are the work of Alexandre-Louis Bellangé (*c.*1823) and were acquired for Windsor Castle by George IV in 1825. They were brought here by Duncannon in 1834, and had to be adapted slightly to fit into the spaces between the plinths of the Corinthian columns. The cut-glass chandeliers are from the Crimson Drawing Room at Carlton House.

More Sèvres vases from George IV's incomparable collection can be seen in this room, notably the garnitures, or groups, of dark blue vases – many of rare and unusual shape – on the chimney-pieces and Bellangé side tables.

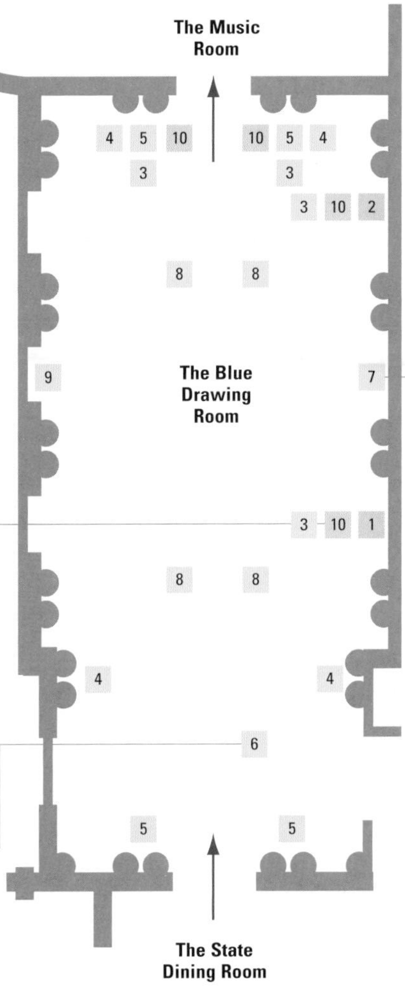

Sèvres porcelain vase (*vase royal*), c.1770

Astronomical Clock, c.1790, by Jean-Antoine Lépine. George IV bought this clock from Lépine, along with several others, at a total cost of £3,250. Made of marble and gilt-bronze, its tripartite design incorporates three dials. The central dial shows solar time (as would be indicated on a sundial) and mean time. The flanking dials give the date, day of the month, signs of the Zodiac and phases of the moon. It is one of the few clocks in the Royal Collection to have retained its original French movement.

PICTURES

1 Sir Luke Fildes, *King George V*, 1911–12

2 Sir William Llewellyn, *Queen Mary*, 1911–13

FURNITURE

3 Four side tables by A.L. Bellangé, marble and gilt-bronze, c.1823; bought by George IV in 1825 for Windsor Castle.

4 Parts of four sets of settees and armchairs by Tatham, Bailey & Sanders and other makers, c.1810–28.

5 Two pairs of candelabra attributed to François Rémond, gilt-bronze, c.1787; probably acquired by George IV for Carlton House in the 1780s. There are two further pairs in the Music Room (see page 65).

6 'Table of the Grand Commanders', hard-paste Sèvres porcelain with gilt-bronze mounts, 1806–12.

7 Astronomical clock with three dials by Jean-Antoine Lépine, c.1790.

8 Set of four cut-glass chandeliers, English, c.1810.

9 Giltwood centre table with a late 17th-century Italian *pietra dura* top.

PORCELAIN

10 Sèvres porcelain vases painted with a dark blue ground, second half of the 18th century.

The Music Room

The Music Room Floor

A spectacular feature of the Music Room is its parquet floor of satinwood, rosewood, tulipwood, mahogany, holly and other woods. This was made by Thomas Seddon and cost £2,400. Inlaid with the cypher of George IV (above), it is a triumph of English craftsmanship and one of the finest of its type in the country.

ORIGINALLY KNOWN AS THE BOW DRAWING ROOM, this room occupies the centre of the garden front of the palace behind the enormous bow-window – an architectural fashion much admired by George IV. It is more disciplined in design than the Blue Drawing Room, with an ingenious and lavishly gilded vaulted and domed ceiling.

The Music Room is entirely Nash's design. It was completed in 1831 and has not been altered since. This is the room where guests, having assembled in the Green Drawing Room, are presented before a dinner or a banquet. Here, too, royal babies are sometimes christened – The Queen's three eldest children were all baptised here in water brought from the River Jordan.

The columns round the walls of the Music Room are of lapis lazuli scagliola; and the walls themselves were originally hung with bright yellow silk, which must have presented a dramatic visual impact in conjunction with the columns. In the tympana at the tops of the walls are three graceful reliefs by William Pitts depicting the Progress of Rhetoric. The subjects are Harmony (north), Eloquence (east) and Pleasure (south). Over the white marble fireplaces are large arched mirrors in concave plaster frames, which complete the architectural treatment of the room.

The carved and gilt Louis XVI seat furniture was acquired by George IV and comes from Carlton House. It was supplied in the late 1780s by Georges Jacob, through the dealer Dominique Daguerre, for Henry Holland's interior of Carlton House. The spectacular chandeliers, of gilt-bronze and cut glass, also come from Carlton House, and are among the most beautiful in the palace (the Carlton House chandeliers were considered at the time of their manufacture to be the finest in Europe).

The windows in the bow, like all the windows on the principal floor of Buckingham Palace, have large-paned glass casements, rather than small-paned Georgian sashes. These were a technological innovation in the 1820s and are among the earliest surviving uses of plate glass in England.

FITTINGS

1 Marquetry floor: satinwood, holly and other woods.

FURNITURE

2 Throne chairs of King George V and Queen Mary, when Prince and Princess of Wales, made for the Coronation of Edward VII in 1902.

3 Small armchairs and settees by Georges Jacob, c.1786; imported into England by Dominique Daguerre in the late 1780s for Carlton House.

4 Boudoir grand piano by John Broadwood & Sons, 20th century.

5 Vase by Pierre-Philippe Thomire, patinated and gilt-bronze, early 19th century; bought by George IV in 1812.

6 Pair of English chandeliers, cut glass and gilt-bronze, early 19th century.

PORCELAIN

7 Soft-paste Sèvres porcelain vases; those on the left-hand chimneypiece supplied by the factory as a garniture in 1764.

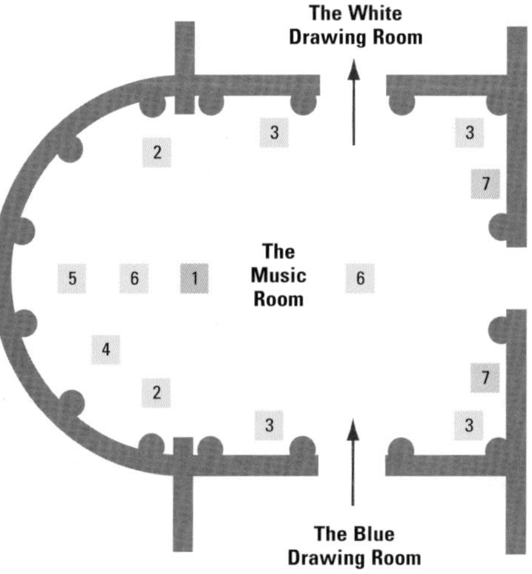

THE WHITE DRAWING ROOM

THE PRESENT WHITE AND GOLD DECORATION OF THE WHITE DRAWING ROOM DATES FROM THE LATE NINETEENTH CENTURY

THE ROOM CONTAINS A SECRET DOOR BESIDE THE FIREPLACE

THE ROYAL FAMILY GATHERS HERE BEFORE MEETING GUESTS IN THE MUSIC ROOM

THE WHITE DRAWING ROOM was originally called the North Drawing Room; in the original decorative scheme the pilasters were of Siena scagliola and the walls covered with gold and white figured damask. The ceiling survives as designed by Nash and combines a tent-like composition with brilliant convex coving and delicate moulded plasterwork by Bernasconi.

There is a further example of William Pitts' plasterwork beneath the ceiling coving in this room. His twelve frieze panels depict the Origin and Progress of Pleasure (they were described by a Parliamentary Select Committee in 1831 as the 'sports of boys'), and cost £800. The individual panels are *Love Awakening the Soul to Pleasure, The Soul in the Bower of Fancy, The Pleasure of Decoration, The Invention of Music, The Pleasure of Music, The Dance, The Masquerade, The Drama, The Contest for the Palm, The Palm Assigned, The Struggle for the Laurel* and *The Laurel Obtained.*

The two white marble chimneypieces in this room, after a design by Flaxman, are also particularly fine. The gilt-framed pier glasses on either side of the fireplace were designed by Blore, and one of them conceals a door from the Royal Closet, through which members of the Royal Family enter the state rooms on formal occasions. The capitals of the pilasters were designed by Nash, and incorporate the Garter Star.

Like the other state rooms, this room also contains magnificent French furniture acquired by George IV. More garnitures of Sèvres vases can also be found here, most of which have a green ground.

RIGHT: Roll-top desk by Jean-Henri Riesener, veneered with fret marquetry and inlaid with trophies and flowers, c.1775. Purchased by George IV in 1825, it may have been made for one of the daughters of Louis XV. It is the most important object in the White Drawing Room.

The four ebony and gilt-bronze cabinets with *pietra dura* panels, placed under Blore's large gilt-framed pier glasses, are adaptations of cabinets formerly at Carlton House. The four French gilt-bronze candelabra, on carved and gilt pedestals supplied by Tatham, Bailey & Sanders in 1811, come from the Crimson Drawing Room at Carlton House.

The gilded and painted grand piano by Erard was bought by Queen Victoria in 1856. It is a reminder of her and the Prince Consort's love of music and the many concerts they held in the state rooms.

PICTURES

1 François Flameng, *Queen Alexandra*, 1908

2 After Joseph Vivien, *François de la Mothe Fénélon, Archbishop of Cambrai*, c.1700

3 After Sir Anthony Van Dyck, *Portrait of a man in armour*, c.1650

4 Sir Peter Lely, *Portrait of a woman*, c.1658–60

FURNITURE

5 Roll-top desk by Jean-Henri Riesener, veneered with fret marquetry and inlaid with trophies and flowers, c.1775.

6 Set of French cabriole-legged armchairs by Jean-Baptiste Gourdin, mid-18th century.

7 Piano by Sébastian and Pierre Erard in a gilded case painted with *singeries* by Francis Richards, mid-19th century; bought by Queen Victoria in 1856.

8 Four ebony and gilt-bronze pier cabinets with early 18th-century *pietra dura* panels.

9 Set of five chandeliers, gilt-bronze and cut glass, English, early 19th century.

10 Set of four French candelabra, gilt and patinated bronze, in the form of a faun or nymph holding cornucopia, late 18th century, on gilded wood pedestals in the form of cranes supplied by Tatham, Bailey & Sanders, 1811; made for Carlton House.

11 Two pairs of candelabra by Pierre-Philippe Thomire, gilt-bronze, early 19th century; bought by George IV in 1813.

12 French patinated and gilt-bronze white marble mantel clock, late 18th century.

13 Two pairs of French patinated and gilt-bronze candelabra, late 18th century.

14 Two pairs of French patinated and gilt-bronze candelabra, late 18th-century; formerly in the Throne Room, Carlton House.

PORCELAIN

15 Sèvres porcelain vases, second half of the 18th century.

16 Pot-pourri stand designed for Brighton Pavilion by Robert Jones, incorporating an 18th-century Chinese celadon vase with *tôle peinte* (painted tin) elements, gilt-bronze mounts by Samuel Parker and a marble base by Henry Westmacott, 1822–3.

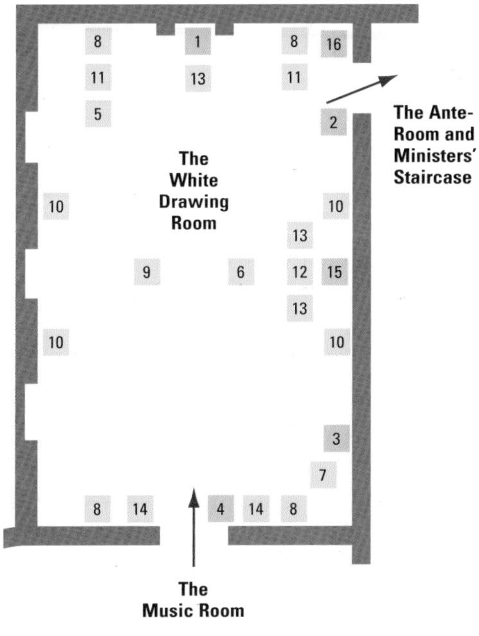

LEFT: Piano by Sebastian and Pierre Erard, mid-19th century. The *singeries* (scenes of monkeys) with which it is decorated were fashionable during this period.

THE ANTE-ROOM AND MINISTERS' STAIRCASE

THE ANTE-ROOM was contrived by Blore as a link between Nash's Picture Gallery and the new private rooms intended for William IV and Queen Adelaide, but never occupied by them. It is given some distinction by its octagonal shape. After the grandeur of the principal state rooms the decoration here is elaborate but small-scale, and the Victorian atmosphere is enhanced by the portraits by Heinrich von Angeli of royal princesses.

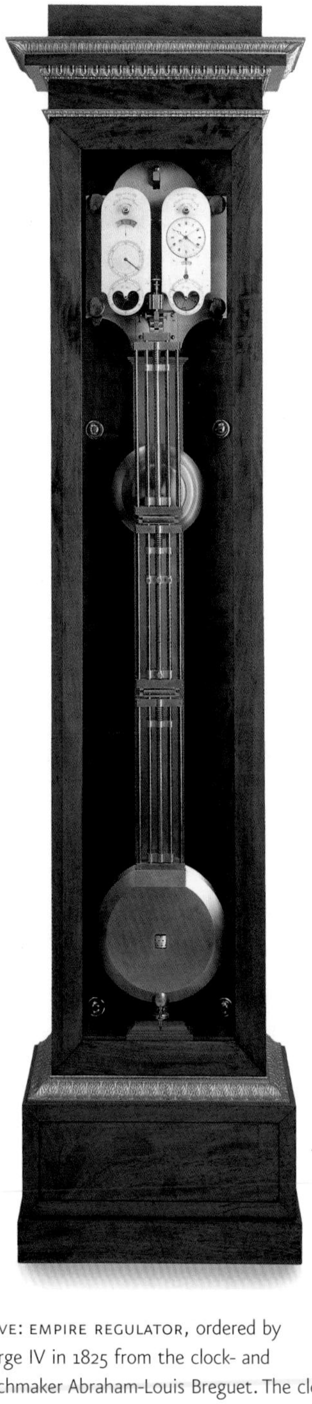

ABOVE: EMPIRE REGULATOR, ordered by George IV in 1825 from the clock- and watchmaker Abraham-Louis Breguet. The clock has two movements whose pendulums act in equal and opposite motion to average their timekeeping.

LEFT: THE MINISTERS' STAIRCASE. At the foot of the stairs is *Mars and Venus* by Antonio Canova, commissioned by George IV in 1815.

The Ministers' Staircase was also introduced by Blore, to give access to the monarch's apartments on the first floor and to improve the circulation at this end of the palace. A sign of Blore's more economical approach to the completion of the palace is the fact that the balustrade here is of gilt lead, rather than the sumptuous bronzework chosen by Nash and George IV for the Grand Staircase. Later the staircase was remodelled by Queen Victoria and redecorated in white and gold in 1902 as part of a sweeping renovation of the interiors of the palace carried out by King Edward VII.

The late eighteenth-century Gobelins tapestries in this area are from the *Amours des Dieux* series and were bought by George IV in 1826. The Empire 'regulator', ordered by George IV in 1825 from Abraham-Louis Breguet, cost £1,000.

At the foot of the stairs is an imposing marble group of Mars and Venus by the Italian sculptor Antonio Canova (1757–1822). It was commissioned by George IV (when Prince Regent) for the Circular Room at Carlton House at the time of Canova's visit to England in 1815. Canova was the greatest sculptor of the age, and George IV owned several examples of his work. This particular piece is seen to best advantage from the Marble Hall, where it forms an impressive focal point to the north end.

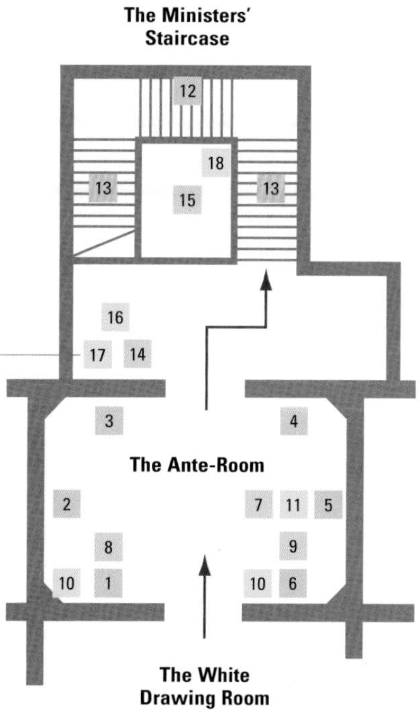

THE ANTE-ROOM

PICTURES

1 Heinrich von Angeli, *Princess Victoria Mary of Teck* (later Queen Mary), 1893

2 Karl Schmidt of Bamberg after Winterhalter, *Prince Albert*, painted on porcelain, second half of the 19th century.

3 Heinrich von Angeli, *Princess Beatrice (Princess Henry of Battenberg)*, 1893

4 Heinrich von Angeli, *Princess Helena (Princess Christian of Schleswig-Holstein)*, 1875

5 Edward Hughes, *The Duchess of York* (later Queen Mary), 1895

6 Heinrich von Angeli, *Princess Louise (Marchioness of Lorne)*, 1875

SCULPTURE

7 W. Reid Dick, *Queen Mary*, bronze, 1938

8 Harry O'Hanlon, *Family of the horse*, bronze, 1988; presented to HM The Queen in 1990.

9 M. Moch, *Two Loons (Canadian sea birds)*, green soapstone, 1990; presented to HM The Queen by the Prime Minister of Canada during the 1990 State Visit.

FURNITURE

10 Two writing desks *(bureaux Mazarin)*, veneered in tortoiseshell with *première-* and *contre-partie* Boulle inlays, late 17th-century.

11 Chest of drawers of Louis XV design, in kingwood parquetry with gilt-bronze mounts.

THE MINISTERS' STAIRCASE

PICTURES

12 John Hoppner, *George IV when Prince of Wales* c.1796

TAPESTRIES

13 Two panels from a set of four from a series of *Les Amours des Dieux*, woven at the Gobelins manufactory after designs by Joseph-Marie Vien, late 18th century; bought by George IV in 1826.

SCULPTURE

14 Mowlm, *Five Innuits tossing a child*, green soapstone, 1977; a Silver Jubilee present to HM The Queen.

15 Antonio Canova, *Mars and Venus*, c.1815–17. Commissioned by George IV following Canova's visit to England in 1815, it was delivered to Carlton House in 1824.

FURNITURE

16 French mahogany and bronze centre table with green marble top, 19th century.

17 Empire regulator ordered by George IV in 1825 from Abraham-Louis Breguet.

18 Barometer and pedestal, attributed to Jean-Pierre Latz, Boulle marquetry and gilt-bronze mounts, c.1735.

THE MARBLE HALL

THE MARBLE HALL. It was originally conceived at Lord Farnborough's suggestion as a sculpture gallery, repeating the arrangement in Farnborough's own house at Bromley Hill, Kent, which had separate sculpture and picture galleries superimposed. The original architectural character of the Marble Hall was more austere than it is now, with plain scagliola walls as a background to marble statues.

THE MARBLE HALL lies underneath the Picture Gallery, and runs from north to south of the main block of the palace. The floor and Corinthian columns are of Carrara marble and match those in the Grand Hall, to which the Marble Hall is spatially connected. Here, as elsewhere, the later gilded decorations were added by Bessant in 1902; the carved and gilded wood swags above the fireplaces, which may in part be early eighteenth century in date, were also placed here then. The two small-scale marble chimneypieces were probably brought from Carlton House when it was demolished.

The marble statues of nymphs were mainly commissioned by Queen Victoria and are by the German sculptors Emil Wolff, Carl Steinhaüser, J. Troschel and Josef Engel.

The portraits in the Marble Hall were arranged by Queen Victoria and show some of her immediate relations, including her mother, the Duchess of Kent; and Ernest, Duke of Saxe-Coburg and Gotha, the father of Prince Albert. They culminate in the official State Portraits of Queen Victoria and Prince Albert painted by Winterhalter in 1859. The arrangement is one of a number of dynastic portrait displays in the palace that were conceived by Queen Victoria and which have survived unaltered down to the present day.

PICTURES

The official portraits of Queen Victoria and Prince Albert of 1859 are preceded by portraits of their relations.

1 Domenico Pellegrini, *Augustus, Duke of Sussex*, c.1804

2 Franz Xaver Winterhalter, *Victoire, Duchess of Nemours* (cousin of Queen Victoria), 1840

3 George Dawe, *Ernest I, Duke of Saxe-Coburg and Gotha* (father of Prince Albert), c.1818–19

4 Franz Xaver Winterhalter, *Victoria, Duchess of Kent* (mother of Queen Victoria), 1849

5 Franz Xaver Winterhalter, *Prince Albert*, 1859; in the uniform of a Colonel of the Rifle Brigade.

6 Franz Xaver Winterhalter, *Queen Victoria*, 1859

7 Eduard von Heuss, *Charles, Prince of Leiningen*, 1841

SCULPTURE

8 Nielsine Petersen, *Christian IX, King of Denmark* (father of Queen Alexandra), 1906

9 Nielsine Petersen, *Louise, Queen of Denmark* (mother of Queen Alexandra), 1906

10 John Francis, *Ernest I, Duke of Saxe-Coburg and Gotha*, 1846

11 Emil Wolff, *Sea nymph with trident*, 1841

12 C. Steinhäuser, *The Siren*, 1841

13 Eduard Muller, *Psyche*, 1861

14 Josef Engel, *The nymph Clotho*, 1860

15 William Theed, *Victoria, Duchess of Kent*, 1861

FURNITURE

16 English carved and gilt gesso tables including two by James Moore, c.1715; with a group of Japanese Imari beaker and baluster vases, 18th and 19th centuries.

17 Spanish damascened steel table made by Placido Zuloaga for Alfred Morrison, 1880; purchased by Queen Elizabeth in 1938.

18 Mantel clock by Benjamin Lewis Vulliamy, gilt-bronze and biscuit porcelain, c.1780.

19 Two pairs of blue-john and gilt-bronze vases by Matthew Boulton, late 18th century.

20 Pair of large vases, cloisonné enamel, early 20th century; given to King George V and Queen Mary by the Emperor of China on their Coronation in 1911.

21 Two from a set of four tripod candelabra by Morel & Seddon, 1826–8.

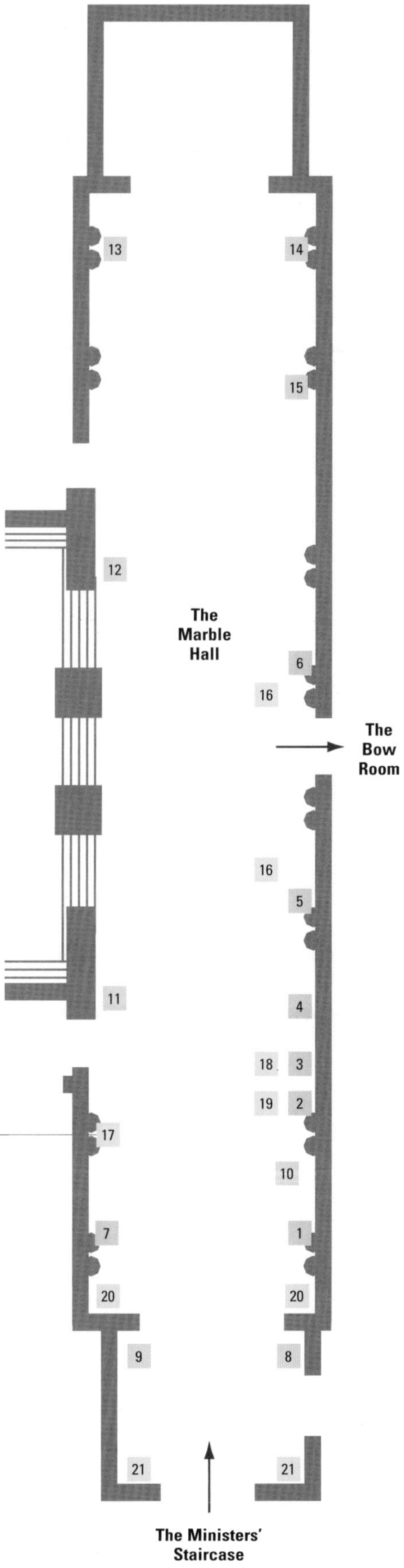

Damascened steel table by Placido Zuloaga, 1880.

The Bow Room

THE BOW ROOM WAS INTENDED TO BE GEORGE IV'S LIBRARY

TODAY GUESTS AT THE GARDEN PARTIES PASS THROUGH THE BOW ROOM TO ENTER THE GARDEN

IN 2000 THE BOW ROOM WAS THE SETTING FOR A BIRTHDAY LUNCH FOR QUEEN ELIZABETH THE QUEEN MOTHER ON THE OCCASION OF HER HUNDREDTH BIRTHDAY

THE BOW ROOM's more restrained classical architecture, with simple Ionic columns, is typical of the semi-state rooms on the ground floor of the palace, which were originally intended as George IV's private apartments.

The pair of dark marble chimneypieces with Empire gilt-bronze mounts by Benjamin Vulliamy date from 1810. They were purchased by Queen Mary and inserted here, where they form a sympathetic counterpart to Nash's architecture. The oval portraits with gilt frames set into the walls were installed at the wish of Queen Victoria in 1853 and again are of European royalty related to the Queen, including the kings and queens of Belgium and Hanover.

The most interesting item in the room is the grand Chelsea dinner service, commissioned by George III and Queen Charlotte as a present for her brother, the Duke of Mecklenburg-Strelitz, in 1763. At the time it was the most ambitious example of English porcelain ever made.

Part of the Chelsea porcelain service of 1763, presented by George III and Queen Charlotte to the Queen's brother, Duke Adolphus Frederick IV of Mecklenburg-Strelitz; and presented to Queen Elizabeth in 1947 by James Oakes.

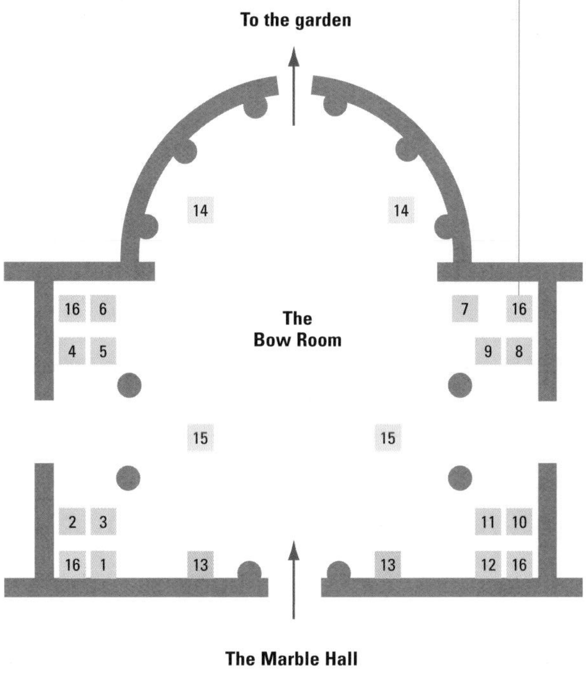

PICTURES

1 Nicaise de Keyser, *Marie Henriette, Duchess of Brabant* (later Queen of the Belgians), 1854

2 Eliseo Sala, *Ferdinand of Savoy, Duke of Genoa*, 1853

3 Franz Xaver Winterhalter, *Augusta, Princess of Prussia* (later Queen of Prussia and German Empress), 1853

4 Franz Xaver Winterhalter, *Ernest, Prince of Hohenlohe-Langenburg*, 1853

5 Franz Xaver Winterhalter, *Prince Leopold* (later Duke of Albany), 1853

6 Nicaise de Keyser, *Leopold, Duke of Brabant* (later Leopold II, King of the Belgians), 1854

7 Carl Oesterley, *George V, King of Hanover*, 1853

8 Franz Xaver Winterhalter, *Frederick William, Grand Duke of Mecklenburg-Strelitz*, 1853

9 Alexander Melville after Winterhalter, *Princess Augusta of Cambridge, Grand Duchess of Mecklenburg-Strelitz*, 1853

10 Alexander Melville after Winterhalter, *George, Duke of Cambridge*, 1852

11 William Corden after Winterhalter, *Princess Mary Adelaide of Cambridge* (later Duchess of Teck), 1847

12 Carl Ferdinand Sohn, *Maria Alexandrina, Queen of Hanover*, 1853

FITTINGS

13 Two chimneypieces by Benjamin Vulliamy, black marble with gilt-bronze mounts, 1810. Commissioned by the Earl of Bridgwater, they were acquired by King George V and Queen Mary.

FURNITURE

14 Pair of English incense burners, mahogany, in the form of a covered urn on a pedestal, late 18th century; bought by Queen Mary.

15 Pair of Regency inkstands, kingwood and gilt-bronze, early 19th century.

PORCELAIN

16 Service, Chelsea porcelain, 1763.

THE GARDEN

THE GARDEN at Buckingham Palace has been described as 'a walled oasis in the middle of London'. Visitors to the Summer Opening at the palace end their tour by walking through the south side of the garden, with splendid views of the west front of the palace, and along the famous lake.

The design of the garden as the visitor sees it today dates back to the conversion of Buckingham House into Buckingham Palace. The new royal residence needed a suitable garden, and George IV appointed William Townsend Aiton, who was in charge of the Royal Botanic Gardens at Kew, to oversee the remodelling of the grounds. Aiton followed the fashion of the times in garden design, introducing naturalistic landscaping and planting to the garden. The two main features for which he is remembered are the creation of the lake and the construction of the 'Mound', a high artificial bank on the south side of the garden, which screens the palace from the Royal Mews.

Since then the garden has undergone a number of further alterations. King George VI and Queen Elizabeth cleared many of the dense Victorian shrubberies, and introduced a wide selection of decorative flowering trees and shrubs. There are now over 200 mature trees in the garden, including many rare specimen trees. A number were planted by members of the Royal Family and are identified by commemorative plaques, or record gifts from different countries of the Commonwealth. The planting in the garden is added to constantly by today's team of gardeners, to introduce new areas of interest and enhance the garden's historic landscaping.

ABOVE: The lake at Buckingham Palace, surrounded by trees and with lawn and flower beds beyond.

LEFT: The garden front, with the two-storey bow-window of the Bow Room (ground floor) and the Music Room (first floor).

RIGHT: In June 2002 the garden of Buckingham Palace was the setting for two Golden Jubilee concerts. Tickets for each concert were allocated by ballot to 12,000 members of the public, and up to a million more watched on giant screens set up in The Mall. Millions more watched the television coverage worldwide. The 'Party at the Palace' became one of the highlights of the Jubilee celebrations.

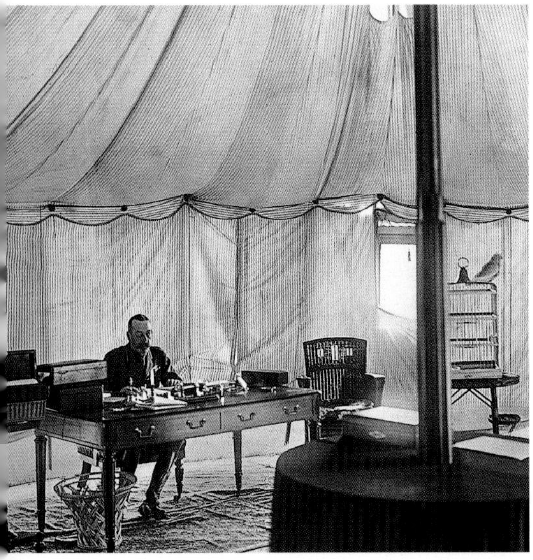

ABOVE: King George V working in a tent set up in Buckingham Palace garden in June 1918. His pet parrot, Charlotte, can also be seen.

The garden is best known as the site for the Buckingham Palace garden parties, which take place on the large area of lawn in front of the Bow Room. Although it is mainly a spring garden, with many spring bulbs and flowering shrubs for that season, including rhododendrons and azaleas, the palace gardeners take great pains to ensure that the immense herbaceous border, to the right of the lawn, is at its most spectacular during the summer, for guests at the garden parties to enjoy.

In recent years, a 'long-grass policy' has been adopted, to encourage wildlife in the garden. As the visitor will see, the lake is now home to over thirty different species of birds, including great-crested grebes, coots, moorhens, shelduck, mallards and geese. Many of these nest in the garden. The long-grass policy has also encouraged wildflowers to flourish in the garden, with a recent survey estimating that the garden contained over 350 separate species, some of them extremely rare.

LEFT: The Queen and The Duke of Edinburgh pause on the terrace outside the Bow Room while the National Anthem is played, before going to meet their guests at one of the Buckingham Palace summer garden parties.

THE QUEEN'S GALLERY, BUCKINGHAM PALACE

THE OPENING OF THE NEW QUEEN'S GALLERY as part of the celebrations of Her Majesty The Queen's Golden Jubilee adds a new and vital element to the history of Buckingham Palace. Many visitors to the palace may not realise however that the tradition of opening royal residences to the public stretches back to the reign of the first Elizabeth, when the earliest descriptions by visitors of the interiors and contents of royal palaces were recorded.

By the early nineteenth century illustrated guides and even 'open days' were being attempted. The Prince Regent opened his beloved Carlton House to the public for three days in June 1811, anticipating 200 visitors every half an hour. (In the event a crowd of 30,000 gathered between Carlton House and St James's Street, causing immense confusion and some injuries.) The state apartments at Hampton Court Palace were regularly open to the public from 1838 and at Windsor Castle from 1845.

Antonio Canova's *Fountain Nymph* of 1815-17 in the Nash Gallery at The Queen's Gallery, Buckingham Palace.

The Chambers Gallery, designed primarily to show prints and drawings and other works on paper.

Sir Anthony Van Dyck's *Charles I with M. de St Antoine*, 1633, in the Pennethorne Gallery. Such enormous paintings can be moved in and out of this room at The Queen's Gallery by removing the lintel and wall above the doors.

Loans of works from the Royal Collection to exhibitions increased steadily during the nineteenth century (Queen Victoria, for example, lent 90 items to an exhibition at South Kensington in 1862). Selected works from the Print Room at Windsor Castle were exhibited at the castle from the 1930s onwards. The opening of the first Queen's Gallery at Buckingham Palace in 1962 appears now as an inevitable progression. Over the next 37 years annual exhibitions were held at the gallery, vastly increasing access, understanding and interest in this exceptional collection.

In that period, air-conditioning and other services at the gallery gradually became out-dated, access for the disabled was always difficult and the gallery itself was seen to be too small to satisfy the expectations of an increasingly discerning public. A larger, more flexible and better-resourced exhibition space was urgently required.

After a limited competition held in 1997, John Simpson was appointed architect. Simpson's designs were for a gallery with over three and a half times the exhibition space of the old, a new shop for visitors to help generate income for the care and maintenance of the Royal Collection, facilities for multi-media in the new e-gallery, education spaces and a lecture theatre, and an air-conditioning system that uses naturally chilled water extracted from a bore-hole in the garden of Buckingham Palace.

Natural materials such as granite, timber, lead and copper are employed in a building which reflects the eclecticism of earlier architects, particularly John Nash and Sir John Soane. Colour and detailing, sculpture and plasterwork, scagliola and cast bronze are used in a manner that will immediately remind many visitors of the state rooms in Buckingham Palace, combining the historic past of the collection with the expectations of the gallery-visiting public today.

Beyond its magnificent entrance hall and staircase, the new Queen's Gallery is divided into four main exhibition spaces. The first of these, the Chambers Gallery, is designed primarily to exhibit works on paper. The second, the Pennethorne Gallery, is top-lit, much like the Picture Gallery at Buckingham Palace, and can be used both as a separate exhibition space in its own right, and as part of larger exhibitions. The Cabinet Rooms, designed for the display of items such as Fabergé, silver and jewellery from the Royal Collection provide smaller, intimate spaces that hint at the excitement of entering a treasury; while the Nash Gallery, contained within one of John Nash's own pavilions at the palace, is large enough to allow the display of paintings, furniture and other decorative arts from the collection within the same space. Access and enjoyment of the Royal Collection is now possible throughout the year on an unprecedented scale.